THE
NORDIC
BAKER

TO K & A

THE NORDIC BAKER

Plant-Based Bakes and Seasonal
Stories from a Kitchen in the
Heart of Sweden

Words and pictures by

SOFIA NORDGREN

Hardie Grant

QUADRILLE

INTRODUCTION

After you've walked past the two big logs, the trail takes a few turns before you reach the big ferns. You have to lift your arms as you push along the path because you don't know what's hiding within their green tendrils, and you certainly don't want to find out.

Then the path becomes steep; you have to trek upwards before you finally reach the old road. To the left is where you collect chanterelles during fall, and to the right is where you find the raspberry bushes. Today, like always, you stop to have a few. When your fingers and lips have turned red, you continue along the road until you hit a crossroads. Here there are lots of rocks more or less under water and you get distracted looking for frogs in the shallows.

A little further down the road something changes. The forest smells different, like a mix of pine and berries and magic. If trolls and elves exist, it must be here they live. You look over your shoulder every other step. Not because you are scared, of course, you just do... You pass a huge ant hill and a few metres ahead there's a tiny pond that is quite hard to see if you don't know it's there. You are close now.

The road continues, but you know that this is where you leave it. You exit on the right side, jump over the little stream and all of a sudden find yourself in blueberry land. There are blueberry bushes as far as the eye can see. You are very close to the lake, and if you walk towards it, you know that cloudberries and lingonberries will reveal themselves, too. You skilfully navigate your way towards the water, where you pick orange berries that look like tiny clouds and taste like the forest. It is silent here.

By the time you've filled your basket with berries, you realize that you've been out for almost three hours. Your fingers are blue, probably your clothes too, and you've got more mosquito bites than you can count. You decide that it's time to go home, but you'll just eat a few more... An hour later it has started to rain (you cannot pick blueberries without it raining, it seems), and you are starting to get cold. Now it's time to go...

As a kid, I spent a lot of time in a little red cabin with white corners, with a lake on one side and the forest on the other. I spent more time outside than inside, building huts hidden in the trees and boats out of bark to play with in the water. Every summer we picked baskets full of blueberries on the fen. The forest was an eternal playground and I found treasures everywhere – I still do. But nowadays, I prefer the edible treasures, and I like preserving them so that they can be enjoyed throughout the year. I also love to search for beautiful things to decorate our home with: fallen branches, a few pinecones, chestnuts, acorns and wild flowers.

As we grow older, we often lose some of our ability to see the magic that nature has to offer. Work, laundry, bills and full calendars often stop us from experiencing nature the way children do. I hope this book will inspire you to go out, forage for whatever is in season and start living more according to the natural world. I hope it will help you to see the beauty of the changing seasons, to love nature and take care of what it gifts to us. And hopefully you will find the inspiration you need to start baking your own bread and delicious bakes with ingredients you've gathered yourself.

With love from a kitchen in the heart of Sweden, *Sofia*.

CHOOSING INGREDIENTS

When shopping for groceries, there are often more options than you
can count. Here, I am sharing my advice on how to make the
best choices when it comes to ingredients and what
to consider when browsing the aisles.

ORGANIC

When possible, I choose ingredients grown
organically. I want to avoid chemicals and
pesticide and herbicide residues for my
own health and for the planet's health. Also,
I personally think that organic products taste
better than non-organic ones.

STONE-GROUND FLOURS

Compared to cheap industrially-milled
flours, where the bran is removed and a lot
of nutrients are lost on the way, stone-ground,
unbleached flours without additives have a lot
more flavour and nutrients. Stone grinding
involves grinding grain between two millstones
– a cold process that is done in one step. This
keeps most of the nutrients within the finished
product, even if it is a white flour. A stone-
ground white flour is often more beige in
colour than an industrially-milled flour. Try
to find stone-ground flour from a local mill,
and always choose organic where possible.

LOCALLY GROWN

Picking fruits, berries and vegetables before
they are ripe, then transporting them in freezer
containers and letting them ripen off the plant
is not what nature intended. The result is fruit
that's hard as stone one day, then rotten the
next. The ones that make it lack flavour and
colour. Avocados are amazing, but buying ten
just to get one that is good and throwing away
the rest is not sustainable for the planet, nor
your wallet. Buying locally grown fruits and
veggies guarantees that what you are eating
is in season, has been allowed to ripen on the
plant and has spent minimal time in trucks.
If you compare a locally grown tomato to one
from another part of the world you realize that
the difference is huge.

SEASONAL FOOD

Eating seasonally goes hand in hand with eating locally grown food. When eating seasonal food, it is often locally grown, and when eating locally grown food, it is definitely in season. To me, buying imported blueberries from the other side of the world in mid-winter is not only insane, it is also very bad for the planet. During the months when we lack fresh produce, we have to turn to the bags of berries we lovingly picked and put in the freezer when the berries were in season. The only time we should use fresh produce is when it is in season.

CHOCOLATE

Choosing chocolate is not easy when grocery stores are filled to the brim with different brands, cocoa percentages and flavours. The best thing to do is to read the ingredients list. You will want this to be as short as possible. Great chocolate should contain nothing more than cacao mass, sugar and cacao butter. If it is flavoured, it should be a natural flavouring agent like dried berry powders, coconut, vanilla, nuts or coffee. Organic and Fairtrade chocolate is better for the environment, and also for the producer.

MY PANTRY

In this section I'm sharing my favourite staples: the ingredients I always have at home. Baking with plants is not difficult, it only requires a few different pantry essentials.

AQUAFABA

We eat lots of beans in our family, but I also keep beans in my pantry for baking purposes. Canned beans are a treasure when baking without eggs – the liquid cooked beans are stored in, called aquafaba, behaves just like egg whites. This makes the aquafaba very useful. You can use all kinds of beans, but my favourite is chickpea broth. Remember that dark beans (like kidney beans and black beans) turn the aquafaba brown. That works just fine when baking something with chocolate, but if you are making a sponge cake, you probably want to use aquafaba from chickpeas or other pale-coloured beans. After removing the aquafaba, use the beans to make hummus or spreads, or use them in your cooking.

FLOURS AND GRAINS

Flour is needed to make almost everything in this book. White flour is used for pastries, while darker flours and wholegrain flours are used for bread. Other grains are mostly used for porridges and granolas. Below is a list of flours and grains I always have at home, and what I use them for.

+ *Plain/all-purpose flour* — mostly used for cakes and other sweets.

+ *Spelt flour* — my favourite flour when it comes to baking bread.

+ *Wholegrain spelt flour* — also for bread. I love to mix white spelt flour with a wholegrain variety.

+ *Rye flour* — a dark, nutty flour, mostly used for bread baking.

+ *Rolled oats* — for porridge, granola, bread, seed crackers and some pastries.

+ *Potato starch* — used for pies, cakes and vanilla custard.

+ *Cornflour/cornstarch* — mostly used for pie fillings.

+ *Psyllium husk powder* — high in fibre and very good at absorbing liquid. This makes it act like a binder when used in baked goods.

NUTS AND SEEDS

Nuts and seeds are very versatile. Use them in bread, bakes and granola to add flavour and a delicious crunch. They are also very tasty to eat as a snack and to use as a topping on your morning oatmeal.

Nuts and seeds are best stored in the freezer. They contain a high amount of fat, which goes bad when stored at room temperature. They are good for a couple of weeks at room temperature, so my advice is to keep as many nuts and seeds as you'll eat throughout one week in your pantry and store the rest in the freezer. Since nuts and seeds don't freeze (they just turn cold), you can use them almost immediately after taking them out of the freezer.

Nuts and seeds I always have at home:

+ *Cashew nuts*
+ *Walnuts*
+ *Peanuts*
+ *Almonds*
+ *Sunflower seeds*
+ *Pumpkin seeds*
+ *Hemp seeds*
+ *Chia seeds*
+ *Flaxseed*
+ *Sesame seeds*

SWEETENERS

There are many options when it comes to sweetening bakes and pastries. Most recipes in this book use caster sugar, but for some recipes, other sugars work better.

+ *Caster/superfine sugar* — used for most pastries and bakes.
+ *Raw cane sugar* — used in some cookies for a caramelly flavour.
+ *Icing/confectioner's sugar* — for frostings and to dust.
+ *Pearl sugar* — mostly used for topping cinnamon buns.
+ *Coconut sugar* — lovely to sprinkle into coffee and perfect for cookies.
+ *Organic pure maple syrup* — used for granola, cookies, bread and everything in between.

FOR FLAVOUR

+ *Pure vanilla powder or vanilla bean paste*
+ *Dried berry powders, like blueberry and lingonberry powder*
+ *Desiccated/dried shredded coconut*
+ *Cocoa powder*
+ *Chocolate* — dark chocolate with at least 70% cocoa solids.

RAISING AGENTS

+ *Baking powder* — used for most cakes and pastries.

+ *Bicarbonate of soda/baking soda* — used mostly for cookies.

+ *Fresh yeast* — for bread and buns. You can use dried yeast instead if you prefer.

HERBS AND SPICES

+ *Cinnamon* — ground and sticks.

+ *Cardamom* — ground and whole pods.

+ *Cloves* — ground and whole.

+ *Ginger* — ground.

+ *Sea salt*

IN THE FRIDGE

+ *Vegan margarine*

+ *Vegan cream cheese*

+ *Plant milks* — oat, soy and almond milk.

OILS

+ *Rapeseed/canola oil* — warm-pressed for baking and cold-pressed for non-heated dishes and bakes.

+ *Extra virgin olive oil* — wonderful to drizzle on freshly baked bread.

KITCHEN ESSENTIALS

For someone who bakes a lot, I don't really own much equipment. We bake all our bread ourselves, yet we do not have a bread machine or stand mixer. My point is that you do not need expensive equipment to start baking. In fact, working a dough by hand gives you a great opportunity to learn how a dough behaves and how much kneading is required to make a great loaf.

Of course, some tasks are rather impossible to perform without assistance, like beating cream for example. However, you can get a long way by owning just an electric hand mixer and a stick blender. I always recommend buying high-quality tools, no matter if they are electrical machines or spatulas. Go for sustainable materials that will last for a very long time, like wood and steel. Steel baking bowls often last a lifetime, and wooden spoons only get better the more they are used.

+ *Wooden spoons* — used to stir doughs and batters.

+ *Electric hand mixer* — for whisking cream.

+ *Stick blender or blender* — for puréeing.

+ *Steel baking bowls* — for combining ingredients.

+ *Spatula* — to stir and to get everything out of the bowl.

+ *Dough scraper* — a useful cleaning tool but also great for dividing dough.

+ *A pair of sharp scissors* — useful for almost everything.

+ *Balloon whisk* — for making things like hot chocolate or vanilla custard.

+ *Sharp knives* — a kitchen without sharp knives is like a car with flat tires.

+ *Pastry brush* — for brushing buns and breads.

+ *Set of measuring spoons* — or a teaspoon and a tablespoon at the least — for measuring ingredients.

+ *Scales/measuring cups* — for measuring ingredients.

+ *A zester or a small grater* — for peeling and zesting oranges or lemons.

+ *Butter knife* — for cutting and dicing margarine.

+ *Cake spatula* — for slicing and serving cake.

+ *Palette knife* — for applying frosting to cakes and bakes.

GET TO KNOW YOUR OVEN

Every oven behaves differently. If you are using your oven frequently, you have probably learned if it is uneven, cooks a little hotter or colder than it is set to, or if it behaves just perfectly. The recipes in this book are adapted to my own oven, and you might have to change the recipes slightly for them to fit yours. Maybe you'll have to use a slightly higher or lower temperature, or turn the baking sheet after half the time. Use the recipes for guidance, but don't be afraid to tweak them a little.

BASICS *grunderna*

EVERYDAY GRANOLA

GRANOLA MED NÖTTER OCH FRÖN

Making your own granola is neither hard nor time consuming. I used to spend a lot of time in the granola aisle at the grocery store, reading labels, comparing different brands, picking one, only to change it one minute later. I often ended up not buying any granola at all. Then I realized that I could make my own. Not only was it cheaper and without additives that are impossible to pronounce, but I also got to make it exactly the way I liked it. This is my basic granola recipe, good as it is, and easy to change depending on what you have at home or what you're craving.

MAKES ABOUT 10 SERVINGS

400g (14oz/4 cups) rolled oats

300g (10½oz/2 cups) mixed nuts and seeds (I like to use hazelnuts, walnuts and almonds)

75ml (2½fl oz/5 tbsp) rapeseed (canola) oil

3 tbsp maple syrup

Pinch of pure vanilla powder, or ½ tsp vanilla bean paste

120g (4¼oz/about 1 cup) dried fruit (I like to use mulberries, apricots and raisins)

Preheat the oven to 150°C/300°F/Gas 2 and line a baking sheet with baking parchment.

In a large bowl, combine the rolled oats, nuts and seeds and stir until well combined.

In a separate bowl, combine the rapeseed oil, maple syrup, vanilla and 2 tablespoons water. Pour it over the oat mixture and stir until very well combined.

Spread the granola out on the prepared baking sheet. Bake in the middle of the oven for about an hour, stirring every 10−15 minutes to make sure it crisps evenly and doesn't burn.

Remove from the oven, allow to cool completely, then toss with your dried fruit.

Store the granola in an airtight container and it'll keep for at least 2 weeks.

GRANOLA WITH DRIED CRANBERRIES

GRANOLA MED TORKADE TRANBÄR

In this recipe, crispy granola meets soft cranberries in the most
perfect combination. The sweetness from the apple juice is
balanced by the sourness from the cranberries –
I love to have this with plant yogurt.

MAKES ABOUT 10 SERVINGS

200g (7oz/2 cups) rolled oats

150g (5½oz/1 cup) nuts of your
choice (I like to use hazelnuts,
cashews and almonds), coarsely
chopped

60g (2oz/scant ½ cup) sunflower
seeds

100ml (3½fl oz/scant ½ cup)
concentrated apple juice

3 tbsp maple syrup

2 tsp ground cardamom

55g (2oz/heaped ⅓ cup) dried
cranberries

Preheat the oven to 180°C/350°F/Gas 4 and line a baking
sheet with baking parchment.

In a large bowl, combine the rolled oats, nuts and sunflower
seeds.

In a separate bowl, stir together the apple juice, maple syrup
and cardamom.

Pour the apple juice mixture over the rolled oats and stir until
well combined.

Spread the granola out on the prepared baking sheet. Bake
in the middle of the oven for about 20 minutes, or until golden
brown, stirring every 5 minutes.

Remove from the oven, allow to cool completely, then toss
in the dried cranberries.

Store the granola in an airtight container and it'll keep for
at least 2 weeks.

OATMEAL

HAVREGRYNSGRÖT

Oatmeal is the perfect breakfast: it takes very little time to make, it's easy to prepare – even at five o'clock in the morning when you are so tired you can barely see – and, most importantly, it's delicious and nutritious. In its simplest form, my oatmeal is made with water, oats and salt, but do use a 50/50 mix of water and plant milk for the liquid, if you prefer. Change the toppings according to the seasons and you'll have a breakfast that you'll never tire of.

SERVES 2

120g (4¼oz/1¼ cups) rolled oats
Pinch of salt

OPTIONAL TOPPINGS, TO SERVE

Seasonal fruits, berries or vegetables
Nuts and seeds
Nut butter
Dried fruit
Homemade jams
Plant milk

Put the rolled oats and salt into a small saucepan and add 650ml (22fl oz/2¾ cups) water.

Bring to a boil, then lower the heat and let simmer for about 3 minutes, stirring continuously, until you have a thick porridge.

Serve with your choice of toppings and a big splash of plant milk.

TOPPINGS

During the spring, summer and autumn months, there are often endless fresh fruits, berries and even vegetables that can be used as toppings on oatmeal. I like to combine fresh berries, with herbs and some seeds or nut butter during this time of the year. One of my favourite combinations is strawberries, finely chopped mint leaves and a spoonful of cashew butter.

It's not uncommon in Sweden to make oatmeal more filling and slightly savoury, by topping it with fresh green peas, kale and roasted buckwheat. Try it and see what you think!

For the winter months, frozen berries or homemade jams are good replacements for fresh fruits and berries. I love the combination of cloudberry jam and sunflower seeds (as pictured).

The topping opportunities are endless, so you'll be able to enjoy wonderful oatmeal breakfasts all year round. Experiment and see what you prefer.

OVEN-BAKED BLUEBERRY OATMEAL

UGNSBAKAD HAVREGRYNSGRÖT MED BLÅBÄR

We eat oatmeal for breakfast 360 days out of 365. It's nutritious, easy to make, and there are almost endless variations to it. Baking it in the oven with blueberries and nuts is one of my favourite methods – it tastes almost like blueberry crumble, and every family member loves it.

SERVES 6–8

Vegan margarine or rapeseed (canola) oil, for greasing

240g (8½oz/scant 2½ cups) rolled oats

900ml (31½fl oz/scant 4 cups) oat milk

3 tbsp maple syrup

½ tsp pure vanilla powder, or 2 tsp vanilla bean paste

1½ tsp baking powder

200g (7oz/1½ cups) blueberries, fresh or frozen

50g (1¾oz/heaped ⅓ cup) hazelnuts, coarsely chopped

Preheat the oven to 200°C/400°F/Gas 6 and grease a 20 x 30cm (8 x 12in) baking dish.

In a large bowl, combine the rolled oats, oat milk, maple syrup, vanilla and baking powder.

Pour the batter into the prepared dish and sprinkle the blueberries on top.

Bake in the middle of the oven for 30–40 minutes until golden and crisp around the edges.

Sprinkle the hazelnuts on top just before serving.

LEFTOVER OATMEAL BREAD

GRÖTBRÖD

Sometimes we make too much oatmeal and have leftovers; we're not
fans of reheated oatmeal in our house, so instead we make bread
out of it. Not only is it a good way of preventing food waste, the
oatmeal also adds a lot of moistness and flavour to the bread.

MAKES 15 BREAD ROLLS

50g (1¾oz/3½ tbsp) vegan
    margarine

250ml (9fl oz/1 cup) plant milk

50g (1¾oz) fresh yeast (or
    25g/1oz dried yeast)

3 tbsp maple syrup

About 300g (10½oz) leftover
    oatmeal

120g (4¼oz/scant 1 cup)
    wholegrain spelt flour

300g (10½oz/2¼ cups) spelt flour

300g (10½oz/2¼ cups) plain
    (all-purpose) flour

Melt the margarine in a saucepan then add the plant milk.
Heat until the milk is just lukewarm (about 37°C/99°F).

Crumble the yeast into a large mixing bowl. Add about half
of the warm milk and stir until the yeast is completely dissolved,
then add the rest of the warm milk and the maple syrup.

Add the leftover oatmeal, wholegrain spelt flour and spelt flour.
Stir to fully combine.

Next, add the plain flour and work the dough with your hands
until it is no longer sticking to the sides of the bowl. Depending
on how much leftover oatmeal you've used, you might have to
add a little more flour.

Divide the dough into 15 pieces and shape each piece to a ball.

Line a baking sheet with baking parchment and place the rolls
on the sheet, leaving a good amount of space between them.

Loosely cover with a tea (dish) towel and place somewhere
warm for about 45 minutes, or until they have doubled in size.
Meanwhile, preheat the oven to 220°C/425°F/Gas 7.

Bake the bread rolls in the middle of the hot oven for about
10 minutes, or until they are slightly golden brown. If you knock
on the base of one of the rolls with your knuckle it should sound
hollow. Remove from the oven and place on a wire rack to cool.

TIP:

If you don't have any leftover oatmeal, you can still make this
loaf. Simply use 60g (2oz/heaped ½ cup) rolled oats, 300ml
(10½fl oz/1¼ cups) water and a pinch of salt and prepare the
oatmeal following the instructions on page 25. Let it cool, then
use in the recipe above.

PANCAKES

PANNKAKOR

No kitchen is complete without a really good pancake recipe.
These ones are large and perfect to cover with homemade jam
and whipped cream. I like to roll these up and bring them
outdoors for a pancake picnic in the garden.

**MAKES ABOUT 10 LARGE
PANCAKES**

240g (8½oz/1¾ cups) plain
   (all-purpose) flour
Pinch of salt
50ml (1¾fl oz/3½ tbsp) rapeseed
   (canola) oil
750ml (26fl oz/3¼ cups) oat milk
Vegan margarine, for frying
Toppings of your choice, to serve

In a large bowl, combine the flour and salt and make a well
in the centre. Pour the rapeseed oil into the well, then gradually
start adding the oat milk, whisking constantly, until you have
a smooth batter.

Place a frying pan over a medium heat and grease it with a
little vegan margarine. When hot, pour about 100ml (3½fl oz/
scant ½ cup) of the batter into the pan and tilt the pan to coat
the base. Cook the pancake for a couple of minutes, or until
the edges start to look golden, then flip the pancake over
and cook for another 30 seconds.

Place the pancake on a plate, and repeat to use the remaining
batter. You can keep the pancakes in a low oven while making
the rest, if needed.

Top the pancakes with your favourite toppings and serve.

SEED AND NUT BREAD

NÖT-OCH FRÖBRÖD

The first time I baked a version of this seed bread was in my turquoise kitchen in my first apartment. It was a rental apartment and the kitchen was hideous. I had invited some friends for brunch and one of them couldn't eat gluten, so I decided to make something special for her. I found a nut and seed bread recipe online and I remember liking it a lot so I kept making it. Over the years I've changed the recipe many times, but this is the way I've been making it for the last couple of years. Maybe it will stay this way, or maybe I'll change it again sometime. You can use it as it is, but don't be afraid to switch up the seeds and nuts, if you like.

MAKES 1 LOAF

150g (5½oz/1 cup) sunflower seeds

70g (2½oz/½ cup) pumpkin seeds

35g (1¼oz/¼ cup) hemp seeds

35g (1¼oz/¼ cup) sesame seeds

70g (2½oz/½ cup) walnuts (or any other nut), finely chopped

45g (1½oz/4½ tbsp) psyllium husk powder

½ tsp sea salt

1 tbsp maple syrup

3 tbsp olive oil

350ml (12fl oz/1½ cups) warm water

Preheat the oven to 180°C/350°F/Gas 4 and line a 1.5-litre (2lb) loaf tin with baking parchment.

In a large bowl combine all the dry ingredients. Add the maple syrup, olive oil and water and stir into a thick paste, ensuring that everything is well combined.

Transfer the dough to the prepared loaf tin and gently press it and smooth it out until flat and even.

Bake for 40–50 minutes until it's browned and crisp on top.

Remove from the oven and allow to rest for 5–10 minutes before lifting the bread out of the tin and transferring to a wire rack to cool further.

Allow to cool completely before slicing into 1cm (½in) thick slices. Store in the fridge for up to 5 days, or it'll keep for months in the freezer.

SOURDOUGH – GET STARTED

BAKA MED SURDEG

Making your own sourdough bread is not hard. All you need is a
sourdough culture, some time and a couple of ingredients. You can
borrow some sourdough starter from a friend, or buy it in a bakery
(some grocery stores now sell them too), but the best thing to do is
to make one yourself – here's how you do it.

SOURDOUGH STARTER

Rye flour (see daily additions
for quantities)

DAY 1

Thoroughly clean a large glass jar and add 25g (1oz/2¾ tbsp)
rye flour and 50ml (1¾fl oz/3½ tbsp) water. Stir with a
fork until you have something that looks like thick pancake
batter. Put the lid on, but leave it ajar. Place the jar at room
temperature, away from any draughts. Let rest for two days.

DAY 3

Add another 25g (1oz/2¾ tbsp) rye flour and 50ml (1¾fl oz/
3½ tbsp) water. Use a fork to stir together. Place the lid loosely
on top and leave the starter for another day.

DAY 4

By now, small bubbles should be visible in the jar. This
means that the starter is active. Feed it once again with 25g
(1oz/2¾ tbsp) rye flour and 50ml (1¾fl oz/3½ tbsp) water
and stir to combine. Leave the starter for another day.

DAY 5

Your sourdough starter is now ready to be used. Take as much
as you need for your bread (page 36), then seal the jar and place
the remaining starter in the fridge (without feeding it).

KEEPING YOUR SOURDOUGH STARTER ALIVE

It's best to keep the starter in the fridge when you're not using it,
where it will last a week without being fed. Once a week (if you
are not baking with it), discard about 100ml (3½fl oz/7 tbsp)
of the starter, then feed the remaining starter with 25g (1oz/
2¾ tbsp) rye flour and 50ml (1¾fl oz/3½ tbsp) water. Stir well
and return to the fridge.

If you are baking with the starter, you do not have to discard any,
since you remove a little each time you make a loaf. You still have
to feed it once a week, though.

BEFORE USING YOUR STARTER

The day before you bake, remove your starter from the fridge and feed it with 25g (1oz/2¾ tbsp) rye flour and 50ml (1¾fl oz/3½ tbsp) water to wake it up.

SOURDOUGH BREAD

SURDEGSBRÖD

If I were to pick only five things to eat for the rest of my life,
sourdough bread would be one of them. The sourdough adds
a lot more flavour to the bread, and when baked until the
crust is really crispy, it's just irresistible.

MAKES 1 LOAF

500ml (17fl oz/2 cups) lukewarm
   water (about 37°C/99°F)
100ml (3½fl oz/scant ½ cup)
   active sourdough starter
   (see page 34)
20g (⅔oz/heaped 1 tbsp) salt
700g (1lb 9oz/5⅓ cups) spelt
   flour, plus extra for dusting

Put the water, sourdough starter and salt in a large mixing
bowl and stir together.

Add about half of the flour and stir until smooth and fully
combined.

Add the rest of the flour and work the dough until the flour
is completely incorporated. If the dough feels loose, add a little
more flour. It should not be wet, but should be a little sticky.

Cover the bowl with a clean tea (dish) towel and leave to rest
on the countertop for 1–2 hours.

Now it is time to start folding the dough. Grab the dough
on one side, lift it and fold it towards the middle. Move the
bowl 90 degrees clockwise and fold again. Repeat this 20 times
until the surface of the dough is very tense.

Line a proving basket with a well-floured tea towel and place
the dough in it. Cover with another towel and place in the fridge
for at least 12 hours, but anything up to 60 hours is fine. A long
rest will give the bread more sour flavour.

Preheat the oven to 250°C/480°F/Gas 9 and put a baking sheet
in the oven to get it really hot.

When the oven is hot, place a sheet of baking parchment on
the hot baking sheet and carefully invert your bread onto it.

Score the top of the loaf with a sharp knife and bake for
35–50 minutes, depending on how crispy you want the crust.

Allow to cool on a wire rack before slicing.

TIP

Adding nuts and seeds can turn the simplest bread recipe
into something even lovelier. Walnuts work especially well
in a sourdough loaf. I like to add 100g (3½oz/⅔ cup) chopped
walnuts along with the flour when making my sourdough to
create *surdegsbröd med valnötter* (walnut sourdough bread),
pictured opposite.

OVERNIGHT BREAD ROLLS

NATTJÄSTA FRALLOR

Is there anything better than a slow morning with freshly baked bread
for breakfast? Unfortunately, it takes quite a while to prepare bread,
and most of us don't have the patience to wait two hours for our
breakfast. The solution? Wake up two hours earlier, *or* make these
rolls that are prepared the night before, and left to rise overnight,
so that all you have to do in the morning is bake them.

MAKES 10 BREAD ROLLS

25g (1oz) fresh yeast
(or 12g/½oz dried)
300ml (10½fl oz/1¼ cups)
cold water
1 tbsp maple syrup
½ tsp salt
110g (3¾oz/¾ cup) rye flour
300g (10½oz/2¼ cups) spelt
flour, plus extra for dusting

Crumble the yeast into a large mixing bowl. Add the cold water
and stir until the yeast has fully dissolved. Next add the maple
syrup and salt and stir again to combine.

Tip in the rye flour and stir until well combined before adding
the spelt flour. Stir thoroughly. The dough should be sticky.

Cover the bowl with cling film (plastic wrap) and place in the
fridge to rest overnight (8–12 hours).

The next morning, preheat the oven to 220°C/425°F/Gas 7
and line a baking sheet with baking parchment.

Sprinkle the work surface with spelt flour and tip the dough
out onto it.

Do not work the dough, just divide it into 10 equal portions
and transfer them to the prepared baking sheet. (Don't worry
too much about shaping them.)

Bake in the middle of the oven for 12–15 minutes, or until
slightly golden.

Let cool for a few minutes, then serve warm for breakfast.
These will keep in an airtight container for a couple of days,
but are best eaten fresh.

NATURE ALL YEAR ROUND

Nature doesn't know what time it is. It does as it pleases and nothing can stop it. We have to obey, and realize that we can never tame the will of nature. When it's time, the first shy spring flowers show up in the ground. The days are getting longer, and the nights shorter.

As time goes by, more flowers will pop up and before you know it, the world has turned pink and smells wonderfully of apple and cherry blossoms. You have to enjoy it while it lasts, because this season is short. But don't become despondent; when one flower fades, another one comes to life.

The days are now longer than the nights and you can run barefoot in the summer evening. It feels like this moment will last forever but, in a month or so, you'll realize that the nights are creeping in again. Before you know it, the first yellow leaves will appear on the trees. The air will change – the soft summer evenings will turn cold and crisp. The trees are now more red than green, until you wake up one morning and realize that all the leaves are gone.

A few weeks later, the first snow will fall and the world will be covered in frost. It's getting colder and your cheeks are turning red. It's completely silent, except for the snow crunching underfoot. Everything is white – the ground, the sky and all the spaces in between. Winter is here and has put a big white blanket over the world. And so the new year arrives. The snow starts to melt – you can hear the dripping sound of snow melting from the rooftops.

Soon the ground will be visible again and before you know it, the first spring flowers will be back. Another year has passed. Another year of nature going to bed, just to wake up again.

SPELT LOAF

DINKELBRÖD

This is our go-to bread. I know the recipe by heart and I have
probably made it hundreds of times. There are few ingredients,
it requires no effort whatsoever and it tastes amazing,
especially when still a little warm.

MAKES 1 LOAF

25g (1oz) fresh yeast
(or 12g/½oz dried yeast)

400ml (14fl oz/1¾ cups)
lukewarm water (about
37°C/99°F)

½ tsp maple syrup or sugar

1 tsp salt

180g (6¼oz/1¼ cups) wholegrain
spelt flour

300g (10½oz/2¼ cups) spelt flour

Crumble the yeast into a large mixing bowl. Add the lukewarm
water and stir until the yeast has fully dissolved. Next add the
maple syrup and salt and stir again to combine.

Add the wholegrain spelt flour and stir until you have a smooth,
liquid batter. Finally, add the spelt flour and stir until you have
a solid dough that is quite sticky, ensuring that there are no
pockets of flour.

Cover the bowl with a tea (dish) towel and place in a warm spot
to prove for 45 minutes.

Line a loaf tin with baking parchment and carefully tip the
dough into the tin.

Cover with the tea towel again and leave to prove for another
20 minutes. Preheat the oven to 250°C/480°F/Gas 9.

Bake in the lower part of the oven for 10 minutes, then lower
the oven temperature to 200°C/400°F/Gas 6 and bake for a
further 20 minutes until golden. If you knock on the base of the
loaf with your knuckle it should sound hollow.

Remove the loaf from the tin and allow to cool on a wire rack
before serving.

RUSTIC BREAD ROLLS

RUSTIKA NATTJÄSTA FRALLOR

Baking these bread rolls requires minimum effort, since they are left
to rise overnight and require no kneading at all. We often prepare
a batch of these on Friday night to have on Saturday,
and they are always gone before noon.

MAKES 10 BREAD ROLLS

15g (½oz) fresh yeast
   (or 7g/¼oz dried yeast)
500ml (17fl oz/2 cups) cold water
½ tbsp maple syrup
1 tsp salt
300g (10½oz/2¼ cups) plain
   (all-purpose) flour, plus extra
   for dusting
360g (12¾oz/2¾ cups) spelt flour
A couple of ice cubes

Crumble the yeast into a large mixing bowl. Add the cold water and stir until the yeast has fully dissolved. Next add the maple syrup and salt and stir again to combine.

Tip in the plain flour and stir until well combined before adding the spelt flour. Stir thoroughly. The dough should be sticky.

Cover the bowl with cling film (plastic wrap) and place in the fridge to rest overnight (8–12 hours).

The next morning, preheat the oven to 220°C/425°F/Gas 7 and line a baking sheet with baking parchment.

Sprinkle the work surface with plain flour and tip the dough out onto it.

Fold the dough in half towards you once, then gently flatten it out until you have a rectangle that is about 2cm (¾in) thick.

Divide into 10 equal pieces and transfer to the prepared baking sheet. (Don't worry too much about shaping them.)

With a sharp knife, make a small cut in the middle of each roll and dust with a little flour.

Place the rolls in the middle of the oven, then immediately pop a couple of ice cubes in the bottom of the oven and close the door (this will give your bread a nice, crispy crust and a soft and moist centre). Bake for about 20 minutes, or until golden brown.

Remove from the oven and allow to cool for a few minutes, before enjoying the bread rolls while still warm. These will keep in an airtight container for a couple of days, but are best eaten fresh.

SEED CRACKERS

FRÖKNÄCKE

Seed crackers are great in many ways. You can add different seeds
every time, based on what you have to hand. They are very quick
and easy to make compared to bread. Plus, they're delicious
— perfect as a little snack or alongside other lunch bits.

MAKES 15-20 CRACKERS

60g (2oz/scant ½ cup) sunflower
  seeds

70g (2½oz/½ cup) sesame seeds

65g (2½oz/½ cup) flaxseeds

30g (1oz/scant ¼ cup) pumpkin
  seeds

55g (2oz/½ cup) cornflour
  (cornstarch)

60g (2oz/scant ½ cup) spelt flour

Pinch of sea salt

3 tbsp rapeseed (canola) oil

150–200ml (5–7fl oz/
  scant ⅔–scant 1 cup)
  boiling water

Preheat the oven to 200°C/400°F/Gas 6 and line a baking sheet
with baking parchment.

In a mixing bowl, combine the seeds, flours and salt. Add the oil
and stir together.

Add 150ml (5fl oz/scant ⅔ cup) of boiling water to the mix and
stir until well combined. If the mixture isn't coming together,
add the remaining water, a little at a time, until it does.

Tip the mixture out onto the prepared baking sheet and, using
a spatula, spread it out into a 3–5mm (⅛–¼in) thick layer and
press it down firmly.

Bake for about 30 minutes, or until crispy, then remove from
the oven and allow to cool completely on the baking sheet.

Once cool, break the cracker into smaller pieces and store in
an airtight container, where they will last for a couple of weeks.

SMALL BREADS

FRALLOR

When I was a kid, you could order bread to be delivered to your door
at the weekends. At that time, there was no such thing as the Internet.
Someone came to your door, wrote down your order on a piece of
paper, and on Saturday morning your fresh bread was delivered.
It was always small bread rolls, and if you were lucky they were
still warm. I loved those breakfasts, and I still love these
"small breads", but nowadays I make my own.

MAKES 20 BREAD ROLLS

25g (1oz) fresh yeast
(or 12g/½oz dried yeast)

500ml (17fl oz/2 cups) lukewarm
water (about 37°C/99°F)

1 tsp salt

2 tbsp rapeseed (canola) oil

420g (14¾oz/scant 3¼ cups)
spelt flour

300g (10½oz/2¼ cups) plain
(all-purpose) flour, plus extra
for dusting

Plant milk, for brushing

Crumble the yeast into a large mixing bowl. Add the lukewarm
water and stir until the yeast has completely dissolved. Next,
add the salt and oil and briefly stir once more.

Add the flour gradually, beginning with the spelt flour and
moving on to the plain flour. Stir until the dough is soft and easy
to work with and there are no pockets of flour left. Continue to
work the dough for a few minutes, kneading it in the bowl with
your hands, until smoother.

Cover the bowl with a clean tea (dish) towel and place in a warm
spot to prove for about an hour. Meanwhile, line a baking sheet
with baking parchment.

Once proved, use a bread scraper or sharp knife to divide the
dough into 20 equal pieces. Dust your hands with flour then
form each piece into a ball – pull the sides down and tuck them
into the bottom of the dough, then use your hands to cup and
roll each into a neat round.

Transfer the rolls to the prepared baking sheet, with a little
space between each, and cover with a tea towel. Leave to
prove for another 30 minutes. Preheat the oven to 250°C/
480°F/Gas 9.

Brush the breads with a little plant milk then bake in the middle
of the oven for 10–15 minutes until golden. If you knock
on the base of one of the rolls with your knuckle, it should
sound hollow.

Allow to cool on a wire rack before serving. These will keep in an
airtight container for a couple of days, but are best eaten fresh.

JAM

SYLT

Making jam is a perfect way to preserve treasures from nature.
When you have eaten as many fresh berries as you possibly can,
turn the rest into jam and save it for the rainy, grey days in March
when the snow is gone and you are just waiting for spring to show
up again. Not many things beat opening a jar of homemade
strawberry jam in the middle of the dark winter.

MAKES 4 X 250ML (9OZ)
JARS (OR I LITRE/36OZ
JAM, DIVIDED AS
YOU WISH)

1kg (2lb 4oz) fresh berries
   (e.g. raspberries, strawberries,
   cloudberries, lingonberries,
   blueberries, blackberries,
   blackcurrants)
250g (9oz/1¼ cups) caster
   (superfine) sugar
1g (a large pinch) sodium
   benzoate

Add the berries to a large saucepan. Slowly bring to a boil while
stirring. When the berries start to release juice, lower the heat,
add the sugar and allow to simmer for a further 10 minutes or
so. Skim off any froth with a large metal spoon.

As the jam starts to thicken, spoon about 100ml (3½fl oz/scant
½ cup) of it into a small bowl. Stir in the sodium benzoate, then
pour the bowl of jam back into the saucepan.

If you prefer a smoother jam, use a fork or spoon to mash and
break up the berries. If you prefer it chunkier, then leave it as is.

Pour the jam into sterilized jars and seal with lids immediately.

Allow to cool, then store. They will last for up to a year if the jars
are sterilized, but do refrigerate after opening.

A SHORT NOTE ON PRESERVATIVES

Whether to use preservatives or not can be debated endlessly,
and I try to avoid them as much as I can. Although sugar is
a great preservative for jams, I try to use as little as possible
and let the sweetness from the berries do the work. If you
are planning on making a large quantity of jam that will be
stored for a long time, I do recommend adding some sort of
preservative (I use sodium benzoate) to prevent it from going
bad and to ensure that all your hard work isn't wasted.

Berries like cloudberries and lingonberries contain natural
preservatives, which prevent them from spoiling, so when
using them there is no need for additional preservatives.

SPRING

vår

ELDERFLOWER SYRUP

FLÄDERSIRAP

If you were to preserve sunshine in a bottle, this syrup would be it.
It's like the grassy meadows, bright nights and the smell of sun-kissed
skin all wrapped up together. I save my bottles of elderflower syrup
for the cold, dark winter, and whenever I need to remind myself of
warmer days I take out one of the bottles and time travel back to the
day when I picked flowers and the entire sunny season was ahead of
me. Serve your elderflower syrup drizzled over pancakes
or ice cream, or use it to flavour cakes.

**MAKES ABOUT
500ML/17FL OZ**

20–25 elderflower heads
(see tip below)
900g–1kg (4½–5 cups) caster
(superfine) sugar
2 organic lemons

Shake each of your foraged flower heads carefully to remove
any unpleasant bugs that you don't want in your syrup.

Put the sugar into a large saucepan with 500ml (17fl oz/2 cups)
water, bring to a boil and allow to simmer for about 5 minutes.

Rinse the lemons and cut them into slices. Add the sliced
lemons and the elderflower heads to the saucepan, bring to
a boil again, then reduce to a simmer for a further 10 minutes.

Turn off the heat and let the syrup cool completely, then put
a lid on the pan and leave to one side for at least 8 hours, or
preferably overnight.

Strain the liquid through a muslin cloth or a fine sieve set
over a large bowl or jug, then discard the lemons and
elderflower heads.

Pour the syrup into sterilized glass bottles and store in the
fridge for up to a month. If you want, you can freeze the syrup.
If freezing it, pour it into plastic bottles instead of glass bottles,
and make sure to not fill the bottle completely to the top, as the
liquid expands as it freezes.

TIP: FORAGING FOR ELDERFLOWERS

Bring a pair of sharp scissors to remove the flower heads.
An elderflower "head" is made of a collection of small stems
and lots of tiny white flowers (pictured). Cut the heads just
below where the smaller stems meet the main stem. Try to pick
them before midday and ensure the flowers have opened and
are full of pollen. Avoid flowers that are still in bud, or those
which have started to turn brown. Do not pick flowers that
have grown close to roads or polluted areas.

MINI PANCAKES WITH ELDERFLOWER SYRUP

MINIPANNKAKOR MED FLÄDERSIRAP

The wonderful thing about pancakes is that you can justify eating them at any time of day. They are perfect for breakfast and brunch obviously, but also for lunch and dinner. These pancakes are small, incredibly fluffy and very delicious, especially when served with elderflower syrup and fresh berries.

SERVES 3–4

300g (10½oz/2¼ cups) spelt flour
1 tbsp baking powder
1 tbsp raw cane sugar
¼ tsp pure vanilla powder, or 1 tsp vanilla bean paste
300ml (10½fl oz/1¼ cups) plant milk
Vegan margarine or vegetable oil, for frying

TO SERVE

Elderflower syrup (see page 54)
Fresh raspberries

In a large bowl, combine the spelt flour, baking powder, sugar and vanilla, and make a well in the centre.

Gradually add the plant milk and 100ml (3½fl oz/scant ½ cup) water and whisk until the batter is very smooth.

Place a frying pan over a medium heat and add a little vegan margarine or oil.

When the pan is hot, spoon small circles of pancake batter into the pan (about 3–4 tablespoons per pancake) and cook for a couple of minutes, until small bubbles appear on the surface. Flip the pancakes and cook for one minute on the other side, until golden, then remove to a warm plate and cover with a tea (dish) towel.

Repeat with the remaining batter, then serve the pancakes with elderflower syrup and raspberries.

SWEDISH CHOCOLATE CAKE

KLADDKAKA

Kladdkaka is probably one of the most popular things to bake in Sweden. It's easy to make, takes almost no time to bake, and it's *very* delicious. If you are a chocolate lover I'm sure you'll adore this thin yet gooey cake.

SERVES 10–12

75ml (1½fl oz/5 tbsp) aquafaba

135g (4¾oz/⅔ cup) caster (superfine) sugar

120g (4¼oz/scant 1 cup) plain (all-purpose) flour

40g (1½oz/5 tbsp) cocoa powder

¼ tsp pure vanilla powder, or 1 tsp vanilla bean paste

1 tsp baking powder

¼ tsp salt

125g (4½oz/½ cup plus 1 tbsp) vegan margarine

2 tbsp cold, really strong coffee (optional)

Whipped plant cream or vanilla ice cream (see page 83), to serve

Preheat the oven to 180°C/350°F/Gas 4 and line a 22cm (8½in) springform cake tin with baking parchment.

In a large mixing bowl, beat together the aquafaba and sugar until white and fluffy (I like to use a hand-held electric whisk for this).

In another bowl, combine the flour, cocoa powder, vanilla, baking powder and salt, then gently fold this into the frothy aquafaba and sugar mixture.

In a small saucepan, melt the margarine over a low heat then add this to the batter along with the coffee (if using). Stir until well combined.

Pour the batter into the prepared tin and bake in the middle of the oven for about 15 minutes. The edges should be crispy, but the middle of the cake should look almost unbaked (it will set afterwards).

Allow the cake to cool in the tin for about an hour, then remove to a serving plate and serve with whipped plant cream or vanilla ice cream.

RASPBERRY THUMBPRINT COOKIES

HALLONGROTTOR

Sweet dough meets tangy raspberries in these delicious cookies
that work well for any occasion. They are perfect for forest
picnics, late evenings with a good book, or to enjoy with
a friend you haven't seen in a long time.

MAKES 30 COOKIES

240g (8½oz/1¾ cups) plain
(all-purpose) flour

90g (3oz/scant ½ cup) caster
(superfine) sugar

1 tsp baking powder

¼ tsp pure vanilla powder,
or 1 tsp vanilla bean paste

200g (7oz/¾ cup plus 2 tbsp)
vegan margarine, at room
temperature, diced

100ml (3½fl oz/scant ½ cup)
raspberry jam (see page 50
for homemade)

Preheat the oven to 200°C/400°F/Gas 6 and line a baking
sheet with baking parchment.

In a large mixing bowl combine all the dry ingredients.

Add the margarine to the dry mixture and use your fingertips
to rub it into the dough until it resembles breadcrumbs, then
start to bring it together. If the margarine is too cold, the dough
will be too crumbly to bring together, so ensure it really is soft
before you start baking.

Divide the dough into 30 even-sized pieces and roll each piece
into a ball between the palms of your hands. Place the cookie
dough balls onto the prepared tray, ensuring that there is a
generous amount of space between each to allow for spreading
in the oven.

Using your thumb, gently press down in the centre of each
dough ball, to create a little hole (don't go the whole way
through). Carefully fill each hole with a little raspberry jam.

Bake the cookies in the middle of the oven for 10–15 minutes
until golden around the edges.

Let the cookies cool completely on the baking sheet before
tucking in. The cookies will keep for up to 2 weeks in an airtight
container, or can be frozen.

[SLOW LIVING]

THE BEAUTY OF ENJOYING
A CUP OF COFFEE IN SILENCE

So much these days is done in a hurry. We are so busy we can't afford to waste a single minute, so we drink our coffee on the go, while we read the news on our smart phones and simultaneously listen to the latest episode of our favourite podcast. I find most people are constantly in a rush, with their heads down, without the time to stop and notice what's going on around them.

In the modern world, when everything is supposed to be done faster and better, I think those small moments to pause and take stock are more important than ever – to be alone with ourselves, just us and our thoughts. When we fill every minute of our day with work, social media and TV, we don't have time to feel. How are you? Are you happy? Tired? Stressed?

Having your whole life stored in a pocket-sized machine is, of course, very convenient. You can do anything anywhere. But it also has its downsides. You do everything, everywhere, all the time. You check your emails while eating breakfast, you scroll through Instagram when the TV show you're watching gets a bit boring, and you check the latest tweets in bed just before sleeping. To stay away from our phones for a longer period of time is hard. But I am convinced we would all benefit from using them a little less, to be more present and to actually live our lives for real, not through our screens or by comparing ourselves to others, or wishing we were someplace else.

Instead of dreaming about travels to faraway places, about the next escape from the everyday, why not try to see the beauty in everything around us? Pay attention to the small things happening around you – flowers starting to bloom in your garden, a frost-covered leaf on the ground, or something as simple as your morning coffee – it's those tiny moments that ground us. Instead of indulging in your daily dose of caffeine on-the-go, make a cup at home, put away everything else (including your phone) and just enjoy that coffee for what it is. Feel the warmth on your hands as you put them around the cup. Take in the smell. Feel the steam rise to your face. Take a sip; how does it taste? Is it nutty or perhaps more chocolatey? Watch the sun and the shadows play on the table. Or is that rain on the window…?

"FIKA"

A moment to sit down and enjoy a cup of coffee and some cake or pastries with friends or family, or just by yourself.

SWEDISH ALMOND CAKE

TOSCAKAKA

This cake is like a deluxe version of the classic sponge cake. The sweet, caramelly almond topping is what makes this cake so special, yet it's very easy to make. The combination of soft and fluffy sponge and crispy topping can be described in no other way than "perfect".

MAKES 1 CAKE

FOR THE SPONGE

150ml (5fl oz/scant ⅔ cup) aquafaba

90g (3¼oz/scant ½ cup) caster (superfine) sugar

240g (8½oz/1¾ cups) plain (all-purpose) flour, plus extra for the tin

2 tsp baking powder

¼ tsp salt

Pinch of pure vanilla powder, or ½ tsp vanilla bean paste

125g (4½oz/½ cup) vegan margarine, plus extra for greasing

150ml (5fl oz/scant ⅔ cup) plant milk

FOR THE ALMOND TOPPING

100g (3½oz/7 tbsp) vegan margarine

70g (2½oz/⅓ cup) caster (superfine) sugar

1 tbsp plain (all-purpose) flour

1 tbsp oat milk

100g (3½oz/1¼ cups) flaked (slivered) almonds

Preheat the oven to 180°C/350°F/Gas 4. Grease a deep 20cm (8in) round cake tin and dust with flour.

Put the aquafaba and sugar in a large mixing bowl and beat until fluffy and white (I like to use a hand-held electric whisk for this).

In a separate bowl, combine the flour, baking powder, salt and vanilla powder, then gently fold this into the frothy aquafaba and sugar mixture.

Melt the margarine in a small saucepan set over a low heat then stir in the plant milk. Pour this into the cake batter and mix everything to combine.

Pour the cake batter into the prepared cake tin then bake in the lower part of the oven for 35−45 minutes, until the sponge is just set. Remove from the oven and allow the sponge to cool completely in the tin.

Once cool, preheat the oven to 200°C/400°F/Gas 6.

Add all the topping ingredients, except the almonds, to a small saucepan and warm over a low heat. As soon as bubbles start to appear, remove the pan from the stove and stir in the almonds.

Cover the sponge with the almond topping then return the tin to the oven and bake on the middle shelf for 20−30 minutes, or until golden brown.

Remove from the oven and once again leave the cake to cool completely in the tin. Once cool, transfer to a serving plate and slice.

COFFEE AND CHOCOLATE CUPCAKES

CHOKLADMUFFINS MED KAFFE

Coffee and chocolate is one of my favourite combinations.
Combining them makes the flavours come to life even more than
when they are enjoyed separately. You can make these any time of the
year, but I particularly enjoy them in early spring, while I'm waiting
for the first fresh produce to show up in the stores and markets
(and in my garden). They are delicious served with coffee.

MAKES 12 CUPCAKES

3 tbsp aquafaba

70g (2½oz/⅓ cup) caster (superfine) sugar

140g (5oz/1 cup) plain (all-purpose) flour

25g (1oz/¼ cup) cocoa powder

2 tsp baking powder

Pinch of pure vanilla powder, or ½ tsp vanilla bean paste

Pinch of salt

75g (2½oz/5 tbsp) vegan margarine

100ml (3½fl oz/scant ½ cup) oat milk

50ml (1¾fl oz/3½ tbsp) cold espresso

FOR THE FROSTING

60–120g (2–4¼oz/½–1 cup) icing (confectioner's) sugar

150g (5½oz/⅔ cup) vegan cream cheese, at room temperature

100g (3½oz/7 tbsp) vegan margarine, at room temperature

20g (⅔oz/3 tbsp) cocoa powder

2 tbsp strong coffee

½ tsp flaky sea salt

Preheat the oven to 180°C/350°F/Gas 4 and line a 12-hole muffin tray with paper cases.

In a large mixing bowl, beat together the aquafaba and sugar until white and fluffy (I like to use a hand-held electric whisk for this).

In a separate bowl, combine the flour, cocoa powder, baking powder, vanilla powder and salt, then gently fold this into the frothy aquafaba and sugar mixture.

Melt the margarine in a small saucepan set over a low heat then stir in the oat milk. Pour this into the cake batter and mix everything to combine. Finally, add the coffee to the batter and stir until smooth.

Divide the batter between the cupcake cases and bake in the middle of the oven for 12–15 minutes until a skewer inserted into the middle of one of the cupcakes comes out clean. Transfer to a wire rack to cool.

Meanwhile, prepare the frosting. Combine all the ingredients for the frosting in a large bowl, starting with the smaller quantity of icing sugar. Use a hand-held electric whisk to ensure the frosting is smooth and well combined.

Now taste it to see if you'd prefer it sweeter. If so, beat in more sugar until you are happy with it. Place in the fridge to firm up while the cupcakes are cooling.

When the cupcakes are completely cool, fill a piping bag with the frosting (or use a zip-lock bag with the corner cut off) and pipe a swirl of frosting on top of each sponge.

Serve straight away or store in the fridge for up to 3 days. The sponges can also be frozen without the frosting.

KLADDKAKA DELUXE

LYXIG KLADDKAKA

Kladdkaka – Swedish gooey cake – is not your average cake. Cakes usually require perfect timing and a bit of patience, whereas this cake is under-baked, takes no time to prepare and doesn't really look that pretty (at least not by cake standards). Yet it's one of the most popular bakes in Sweden. Try it, and you will understand why. Compared to the *kladdkaka* on page 59, this is much thicker and fluffier.

MAKES 1 CAKE

150ml (5fl oz/scant ⅔ cup) aquafaba

180g (6¼oz/scant 1 cup) caster (superfine) sugar

150g (5½oz/1 cup plus 2 tbsp) plain (all-purpose) flour

40g (1½oz/5 tbsp) cocoa powder

2 tsp baking powder

¼ tsp salt

100ml (3½fl oz/scant ½ cup) rapeseed (canola) oil

Icing (confectioner's) sugar, for dusting

Ice cream (see page 83) or whipped plant cream, to serve

Preheat the oven to 200°C/400°F/Gas 6 and line a 20cm (8in) round cake tin with baking parchment.

In a large mixing bowl, beat together the aquafaba and sugar until white and fluffy (I like to use a hand-held electric whisk for this).

In a separate bowl, combine the flour, cocoa powder, baking powder and salt, then gently fold this into the frothy aquafaba and sugar mixture.

Add the rapeseed oil and stir until smooth, then pour the batter into the prepared tin.

Bake in the middle of the oven for 13–15 minutes until firm around the edges and dry to the touch, but a skewer inserted into the centre of the cake should still come out wet – the cake will set further as it cools. Remove from the oven and leave to cool completely in the tin.

Once cool, dust the top of the cake with a little icing sugar before serving with ice cream or whipped plant cream.

RASPBERRY PANCAKE CAKE

PANNKAKSTÅRTA

Eating a piece of this cake is like time travelling back to my childhood and the first day of summer vacation. There is a little table with two chairs in a corner of the garden, just beneath the plum tree. The table is set with a gingham table cloth and a cake stand is ready with the most delicious cake – layers of pancakes, whipped cream and raspberry jam. You could even add a drizzle of chocolate, if you like.

MAKES 1 CAKE

FOR THE PANCAKES

240g (8½oz/1¾ cups) plain (all-purpose) flour

Pinch of salt

50ml (1¾fl oz/3½ tbsp) rapeseed (canola) oil, plus extra for greasing

750ml (26fl oz/3¼ cups) oat milk

100g (3½oz) dark chocolate (70% cocoa solids or higher), plus 25g (1oz), to serve

FOR THE FILLING

500g (1lb 4oz/4 cups) fresh or frozen raspberries (or raspberry jam if you prefer), plus extra for decorating

200ml (7fl oz/scant 1 cup) vegan whipping cream

Begin with the pancakes. In a large bowl, combine the flour and salt and make a well in the centre. Pour the rapeseed oil into the well, then gradually start adding the oat milk, whisking constantly, until you have a smooth batter.

Place a frying pan over a medium heat and grease it with a little oil. When hot, pour about 75ml (2½fl oz/5 tbsp) of the batter into the pan and tilt the pan to coat the base. Cook the pancake for a couple of minutes, or until the edges start to look golden, then flip the pancake over and cook for another 30 seconds.

Place the pancake on a plate or wire rack, and repeat until you have used up all the remaining batter. While you wait for the pancakes to cool down, prepare the filling.

Place the berries in a blender or food processor and blitz until you have a smooth purée. (Skip this step if you are using jam.)

In a large bowl, whisk the whipping cream until fluffy using a hand-held electric whisk.

Make sure all the pancakes have completely cooled before you start building your cake, otherwise the cream will melt and all you'll have left is a mess. Place a pancake on a plate or cake stand. Spread a thin layer of the raspberry purée on top of the pancake, going right to the edges. Then, add a layer of the whipped cream (again, make sure to cover the entire pancake), before placing another pancake on top.

Repeat with the remaining pancakes until you have one pancake left. Place this final pancake on top of the cake, then top with the reserved raspberries.

Place your chocolate in a small heatproof bowl set over a pan of barely simmering water. Once melted, drizzle the chocolate all over the top of your pancake cake.

Finally, grate over the remaining chocolate, serve and enjoy!

RHUBARB COMPOTE

RABARBERKOMPOTT

During rhubarb season, we always have a big jar of rhubarb compote
in the fridge. We use it on our breakfast porridge, on chia puddings
and sometimes we just grab a spoon and have it straight from the jar.
If you want, you can add a handful of strawberries to the compote too;
their sweetness balances the sourness of the rhubarb perfectly.

MAKES 300G (10½OZ)

500g (1lb 2oz) rhubarb stalks
3 tbsp maple syrup
2 tbsp raw cane sugar
¼ tsp pure vanilla powder,
    or 1 tsp vanilla bean paste

Cut the rhubarb stalks into 5mm−1cm (¼−½in) slices.

In a large saucepan, combine the rhubarb, maple syrup,
cane sugar, vanilla powder or paste and 100ml (3½fl oz/
scant ½ cup) water. Bring to a boil, then lower the heat
and simmer for about 10 minutes until the rhubarb is
soft and the mixture has thickened a little.

Allow the compote to cool, then transfer to clean jars
or an airtight container. This will keep in the fridge for
up to 5 days.

A PASTEL EXPLOSION OF DELICATE FLOWERS THAT
FEELS LIKE WALKING THROUGH COTTON CANDY

RHUBARB GALETTE

RABARBERGALETTE

When the first rhubarb appears in the garden, or in your local store,
you know that spring has arrived for real. The days are longer,
the sun feels warmer and very soon nature will turn into a
pastel explosion of flowers. This rhubarb galette is perfect
to celebrate the arrival of spring.

SERVES 6

180g (6¼oz/1⅓ cups) plain
(all-purpose) flour, plus extra
for dusting

1 tbsp caster (superfine) sugar

Pinch of salt

150g (5½oz/⅔ cup) vegan
margarine, chilled

1–3 tbsp ice cold water

Oat milk, for brushing

Vanilla ice cream (see page 83),
to serve

FOR THE FILLING

200–250g (7–9oz) rhubarb stalks

3–4 tbsp caster (superfine) sugar

2 tsp potato starch

¼ tsp pure vanilla powder,
or 1 tsp vanilla bean paste

Pinch of salt

2 tbsp lemon juice

To make the dough, combine the flour, sugar and salt in a large
bowl. Dice the cold margarine and rub it into the flour using
your fingertips until the mixture resembles breadcrumbs.
Add the ice cold water, 1 tablespoon at a time, until the dough
just comes together, then form it into a ball with your hands.

Shape the dough into a disc, wrap in cling film (plastic wrap)
and let it rest in the fridge for at least one hour. Leaving it
overnight is absolutely fine too. You may need to let the dough
warm up for a few moments on the countertop before you start
baking with it, to ensure that it's workable.

Preheat the oven to 200°C/400°F/Gas 6 and line a baking sheet
with baking parchment.

On a lightly floured surface, roll out the dough to a circle about
3mm (⅛in) thick. Transfer it to the prepared baking sheet.

Trim the ends of the rhubarb and slice the stalks into 3–4cm
(1¼–1½in) lengths, then place them in a large bowl.

Add the remaining filling ingredients to the bowl and toss
everything together to coat the rhubarb.

Arrange the rhubarb pieces in a single layer in a pretty pattern
on top of the dough, leaving a 4cm (1½in) border around the
edge. Fold the bare edge of the dough over the rhubarb filling
and gently press to seal.

Brush the edges of the galette with oat milk, then place it in
the middle of the hot oven and bake for about 35 minutes,
until the edges are golden brown and the rhubarb is soft.

Serve warm or cold with my vanilla ice cream.

RHUBARB BLONDIES

RABARBERBLONDIES

Even though rhubarb is available for quite a long period of time, I like to preserve some so I can enjoy the wonderful flavour even when there are no more stalks in my garden. Rhubarb blondies are delicious when still warm from the oven, but also freeze very well so you can enjoy them out of rhubarb season, too.

MAKES 15–20 BLONDIES

150ml (5fl oz/scant ⅔ cup) aquafaba

225g (8oz/1 cup plus 2 tbsp) caster (superfine) sugar

150g (5½oz/⅔ cup) vegan margarine

250ml (9fl oz/1 cup) plant milk

480g (1lb 1oz/3⅔ cups) plain (all-purpose) flour

1 tbsp baking powder

¼ tsp pure vanilla powder, or 1 tsp vanilla bean paste

500g (1lb 2oz) rhubarb stalks

30g (1oz/3 tbsp) pearl sugar

15–20g (½–⅔oz/¼ cup) flaked (slivered) almonds

Preheat the oven to 200°C/400°F/Gas 6 and line a 25 x 35cm (10 x 14in) baking tin with baking parchment.

In a large bowl, beat together the aquafaba and sugar until fluffy (I like to use a hand-held electric whisk for this).

Melt the margarine in a saucepan set over a low heat then stir in the plant milk. Pour this into the frothy aquafaba and sugar mixture and stir to combine.

In a separate bowl, combine the flour, baking powder and vanilla, then gently fold this into your wet mixture until combined. Pour the batter into the prepared baking tray.

Cut the rhubarb stalks into small chunks and dot them evenly over the cake batter, then sprinkle the blondies with the pearl sugar and flaked almonds.

Bake in the middle of the oven for about 20 minutes, until golden, then remove from the oven and allow to cool in the tin.

Once cool, lift the blondies out of the tin and cut into squares. Enjoy as they are, or serve with vanilla ice cream (page 83) or custard (page 136) for dessert.

VANILLA CUSTARD HEARTS

VANILJHJÄRTAN

Crispy, heart-shaped pastries with a hidden treasure of vanilla custard
– these are not just wonderfully delicious, but also beautiful to look at.
Making them takes a little time and effort but if you allow yourself to
enjoy the process then you will delight in the result even more.
To make these, you'll need small heart-shaped tins, which you can
find in kitchen supplies stores, but you can also use mini tart cases.

MAKES 6 VANILLA HEARTS

FOR THE PASTRY

120g (4¼oz/scant 1 cup) plain
  (all-purpose) flour

40g (1½oz/4 tbsp) potato starch

30g (1oz/3 tbsp) caster (superfine)
  sugar

¼ tsp pure vanilla powder,
  or 1 tsp vanilla bean paste

Pinch of salt

100g (3½oz/7 tbsp) vegan
  margarine, chilled, plus extra
  for greasing

FOR THE CUSTARD

150ml (5½fl oz/scant ⅔ cup)
  oat milk

1 tbsp potato starch

Pinch of salt

½ tsp pure vanilla powder,
  or 2 tsp vanilla bean paste

2 tbsp caster (superfine) sugar

10g (⅓oz/2 tsp) vegan margarine

Icing (confectioner's) sugar,
  for dusting

Start by making the pastry. Combine the flour, potato starch, sugar, vanilla and salt in a large bowl. Dice the cold margarine and rub it into the flour using your fingertips until the mixture resembles breadcrumbs. At this stage, it might come together – if not, add ½ teaspoon of ice cold water at a time, until the dough just comes together, then shape it into a ball with your hands. Wrap the pastry in cling film (plastic wrap) and place in the fridge to rest for about an hour.

Meanwhile, prepare the custard. In a saucepan, combine the oat milk and potato starch. Stir continuously over a medium heat until it thickens. Remove the saucepan from the stove and whisk in the salt, vanilla, sugar and margarine, until combined, then set aside to cool.

Preheat the oven to 220°C/425°F/Gas 7. Generously grease six 6 x 7cm (2½ x 2¾in) heart-shaped tins (or mini tart cases) with margarine.

On a lightly floured surface, roll out the dough until it is 3mm (⅛in) thick. Using a tin as a guide, cut out six heart-shaped pieces of dough that are a little bigger than the tin. Repeat, so that you have six heart-shaped lids that are the same size as the tin.

Line the tins with your slightly larger heart-shaped dough pieces, pressing with your thumbs to make sure the dough sticks to the bottom and sides of each tin. Add about a tablespoon of vanilla custard to each, then top each with a pastry lid. Seal the edges by gently pressing down with your thumb, then remove any excess pastry with a sharp knife.

Bake in the lower part of the oven for 12–15 minutes, or until slightly golden. When baked, allow to cool for a few minutes in the tins, then carefully remove from the tins and place the hearts on baking parchment set over a wire rack and allow to cool completely. Sprinkle with icing sugar before serving.

NO-CHURN VANILLA
ICE CREAM

VANILJGLASS UTAN GLASSMASKIN

If I were to keep just one flavour of ice cream in my freezer,
I'd definitely go for vanilla. It goes well with everything and it's very
tasty on its own. Making your own ice cream is easy, requires no
special equipment and you need only a few ingredients.

MAKES 1 LITRE (35OZ)

250g (9oz/1 cup) vegan condensed
milk (page 124 for homemade)

¼ tsp pure vanilla powder,
or 1 tsp vanilla bean paste

300ml (10½fl oz/1¼ cups) vegan
whipping cream

60g (2oz/½ cup) icing
(confectioner's) sugar

In a medium bowl combine the condensed milk and vanilla.

In a separate, larger bowl beat the whipping cream using
a hand-held electric whisk, until stiff peaks form.

Pour in the vanilla condensed milk, then sift in the icing
sugar, and continue to beat for a further few minutes until
completely combined.

Pour the ice cream mixture into a freezable container, seal
and place in the freezer for at least 4 hours.

THE CALMING POWER OF
TREES AND WATER

Nature has always been my biggest source of inspiration, as well as the most important place for rest, recovery and clearing my head. There's something about walking among trees that are 100 years older than me that is very calming, I think. It's like they know everything that is worth knowing about this world and that thought alone always make me feel better. I also tend to find answers to things I'm stuck with. When you let go of things that trouble you and take a break, you often find the solution popping up in your head when you least expect it. I seem to have those moments when I'm outdoors, especially when in the forest.

I sit down, look up at the tree crowns swaying above, watch the clouds pass by, and just breathe the fresh air. Or I look to the forest floor and realize that there is an entire world down there: tiny flowers, a beetle running around, a smooth chestnut, or a colourful autumn leaf covered with tiny water droplets that reflect everything there is to see around you.

The beauty of nature is in the little things – the bumblebees buzzing around searching for flowers, the weeds covering the ditches, dandelion seeds flying around in the air like miniature parachutes. Nature does not wait for you to see its beauty. It does what it does, whether you are watching or not. I find that very comforting – like a warm hug from my grandmother. Nature is always there when we need it. And we do need it.

We are made to be outdoors. Humans have always been outdoors, searching for food and shelter. Foraging runs in our blood; it comes naturally at a young age. The mind can wander while the hands do the work. It is easy to lose track of time when all you have to think about is which blueberry bush to go to next. We are made for fresh air and berry-stained hands.

Being close to water has always been very important to us, too. Here, food is more available, the view is clear and far-reaching. In the modern world, this might not be as important as it was back in the old days. However, most of us still love to be close to water. People pay a ridiculous amount of money for a house with a nice view of the sea. There is something about water that is very calming. This is true for me too. Few things make me as calm as the ocean. Water as far as the eye can see. Nothing but waves hitting the shore. I can spend hours there, just watching it, listening.

There is also always something going on: a fish jumping up and diving back down into the water again; a couple of water striders roaming the surface; perhaps even a moose searching to quench his thirst. Even at times when you are alone, the water itself always fascinates – crashing waves in a storm, a ripple on a summer evening. Water reflects the many shades of nature.

Whether I'm by the ocean, in the forest or in the mountains does not matter. Being in nature does wonders for my well-being. My lungs are filled with crisp air, my cheeks are warmed by the sun, and my feet touch the ground. I feel very connected to the planet, like I am part of it, which I, of course, am. Like we all are. Leave the emails, mountains of laundry and deadlines at home and just be. Breathe. Pay attention.

I am very fortunate to live close to the ocean. Every day I take my son and walk down to watch the waves hitting the shore. I listen to the sound, let the smell of salt water fill my nose and watch the water obey the wind. My son loves it too.

During the weekends we often pack a rucksack with sandwiches, hot chocolate and cinnamon buns and head out to the forest. We hike and play with sticks and rocks, and when our stomachs begin to rumble, we sit down on the nearest rock or tree stump to eat. We eat, play and explore, and when we are tired, we go back home. Afterwards, it always feels as though nature has just given us a big squeeze, and we can rest easy.

Nature does not wait for you to see its beauty. It does what it does, whether you are watching or not.

SUMMER

sommar

MINI CHERRY PIES

MINIKÖRSBÄRSPAJER

My mum is the queen of pies, both sweet and savoury.
Everything I know about pie making, I have learned from her.
The idea for these cherry pies is also inspired by her. She made this
cherry crumble pie once, which was outstanding, and I've tried to
replicate those flavours here. These are perfect to pack into a picnic
basket and enjoy on any outdoor adventure.

MAKES 4 SMALL PIES

180g (6¼oz/1⅓ cups) plain
(all-purpose) flour, plus extra
for dusting

1 tbsp caster (superfine) sugar

Pinch of salt

150g (5½oz/⅔ cup) vegan
margarine, chilled

2–3 tbsp cold water

Plant milk, for brushing

FOR THE FILLING

450g (1lb/3 cups) fresh cherries,
pitted

90g (3¼oz/scant ½ cup) caster
(superfine) sugar

2 tbsp cornflour (cornstarch)

2 tbsp lemon juice

Pinch of salt

To make the dough, combine the flour, sugar and salt in a large
bowl. Dice the cold margarine and rub it into the flour using
your fingertips until the mixture resembles breadcrumbs. Add
the ice cold water, 1 tablespoon at a time, until the dough just
comes together, then form it into a ball with your hands.

Shape the dough into a disc, wrap in cling film (plastic wrap)
and let it rest in the fridge for at least one hour. Leaving it
overnight is absolutely fine too. You may need to let the dough
warm up for a few moments on the countertop before you start
baking with it, to ensure that it's workable.

Meanwhile, make the filling. Put all the ingredients in a saucepan,
set it over a low heat and simmer for about 5 minutes, stirring
continuously. Put to one side and allow to cool completely.

Preheat the oven to 200°C/400°F/Gas 6 and line a baking sheet
with baking parchment.

Divide the dough in half; one portion will be used to make the
bases, and the other will be used to make the lids.

On a floured surface, roll out one portion to about 3mm (⅛in)
thick and cut out four circles 12cm (4½in) in diameter using a
large cookie cutter or small plate as a guide. Transfer the dough
circles to the prepared baking sheet.

Divide the cherry filling evenly between the four dough circles,
leaving a 2cm (¾in) border around the edges.

Roll out the remaining dough to a rectangle 3mm (⅛in) thick;
this will be used to make the lids.

CONTINUED...

CONTINUED...

To make a closed lid, cut out four circles from your dough that are about 18cm (7in) in diameter and use a small cookie cutter or the end of a piping nozzle to remove holes from each circle (as pictured), to allow the steam to escape. Place the lid over each filled pie, then use your thumb to press and seal the lid to the base.

To make a striped lid, cut small strips of dough, about 18cm (7in) long and 1cm (½in wide), and evenly arrange them in patterns over the top of your cherry filling (as pictured). Use your thumb to press and seal the strips to the base, then trim off any excess using a sharp knife.

To make a latticed lid, cut out 10 small strips of dough for each pie, each about 18cm (7in) long and 1cm (½in wide). Evenly place five dough strips over one of your filled pies, parallel to each other. Fold back every other strip and place a new strip of dough perpendicular to the original strips, then return the folded-back strips to their starting position. Now, fold back the opposite strips to those you folded back before and place a new strip perpendicular to them. Once again, return the folded-back strips to their starting position. Repeat until the lattice crust covers the pie. Use your thumb to press and seal the strips to the base, then trim off any excess using a sharp knife. Repeat with the remaining pies.

Brush the lid of your pies with plant milk and bake in the middle of the oven for 15–20 minutes, until golden. Allow to cool on the baking sheet, then enjoy.

STRAWBERRY AND BLACKBERRY CRUMBLE

SMULPAJ MED JORDGUBBAR OCH BJÖRNBÄR

To me, nothing says summer more than fresh berries. I can eat countless fresh berries during the summer season, but I also make sure to bake a lot with them. Berry pies are a favourite in our house, like this one with strawberries and blackberries. It also works just fine with frozen berries, so if you have some left in the freezer and want crumble in the middle of the winter, go for it.

SERVES 4–6

500g (1lb 2oz) mixture of strawberries and blackberries

1 tbsp potato starch

20g (⅔oz/2 tbsp) caster (superfine) sugar

¼ tsp pure vanilla powder, or 1 tsp vanilla bean paste

Vanilla ice cream (page 83), to serve

FOR THE CRUMBLE

80g (2¾oz/¾ cup) rolled oats

60g (2oz/scant ½ cup) plain (all-purpose) flour

100g (3½oz/7 tbsp) vegan margarine, chilled and diced

70g (2½oz/⅓ cup) caster (superfine) sugar

Pinch of salt

Preheat the oven to 180°C/350°F/Gas 4.

Put all the ingredients for the crumble into a large bowl and use your fingertips to rub everything together until it resembles a crumbly dough.

Halve the strawberries and add them to a 20cm (8in) baking dish together with the blackberries.

In a small bowl, combine the potato starch, sugar and vanilla, then sprinkle this over the berries. Toss to coat the fruit.

Sprinkle the crumble evenly over the top of the berries, then bake for about 35 minutes in the middle of the oven. The crumble is done when the top is golden brown.

Remove from the oven, allow to stand for 10–15 minutes, then serve with ice cream.

MIDSUMMER CAKE

MIDSOMMARTÅRTA

A summery and tasty cake made with just sponge, whipped cream and
fresh berries. Since Midsummer is all about celebrating the arrival of
the summer season, what could be more perfect than a simple cake
where the berries are the focus?

SERVES 8–12

150ml (5fl oz/scant ⅔ cup)
  aquafaba

90g (3¼oz/scant ½ cup) caster
  (superfine) sugar

100g (3½oz/7 tbsp) vegan
  margarine, plus extra for
  greasing

150ml (5fl oz/scant ⅔ cup)
  plant milk

240g (8½oz/1¾ cups) plain
  (all-purpose) flour

2 tsp baking powder

¼ tsp pure vanilla powder,
  or 1 tsp vanilla bean paste

Pinch of salt

250ml (9fl oz/1 cup) vegan
  whipping cream

100ml (3½fl oz/scant ½ cup)
  strawberry jam (see page
  50 for homemade)

500g (1lb 2oz) fresh berries
  (strawberries, raspberries,
  blackberries, blackcurrants,
  redcurrants, wild strawberries),
  to decorate

Preheat the oven to 180°C/350°F/Gas 4 and grease and
line a deep, round cake tin 15–18cm (6–7in) in diameter,
with a depth of at least 10cm (4in).

Put the aquafaba and sugar in a mixing bowl and beat with a
hand-held electric whisk until white and fluffy.

Melt the margarine in a small saucepan set over a low heat,
then stir in the plant milk. Pour this into the aquafaba and sugar
mixture and stir to combine.

In a separate bowl, combine the flour, baking powder, vanilla
and salt, then gently fold this into your wet mixture until no
clumps of flour are visible.

Pour the batter into the prepared cake tin and bake in the lower
part of the oven for 50–60 minutes until the sponge is risen and
lightly golden. A skewer inserted into the middle should come
out clean.

Remove from the oven, allow to cool for about 15 minutes in the
tin, then remove the sponge from the tin and transfer to a wire
rack to cool completely. Once cool, cut in half horizontally so
that you have two even sponge layers.

For the filling, place the whipping cream in a large bowl and
beat with a hand-held electric whisk until stiff peaks form –
this usually takes about 10 minutes.

To assemble your cake, place one sponge on a serving plate and
spread with half the strawberry jam, right to the edges. Cover
this with a generous amount of cream.

Spread the top of the other sponge with the remaining
strawberry jam, then place this (jam side up) on top of your cake.
Top with lots more cream and then adorn with fresh berries.

FLOWERS DRAPE THE MEADOWS IN
BRIGHT COLOURS, AND BAREFOOT
WE RUN INTO THE WARM NIGHT

[SLOW LIVING]

SUMMER MEADOWS, DANCING FAIRIES AND ENDLESS STRAWBERRIES

My love for nature came early. In fact, I was more or less born into it. In the early '50s, my grandfather built a cabin in the woods, right by a very small lake. He built it by hand, which at that time meant dragging logs through the forest – a distance of about 500 metres. It also meant digging the ground with nothing but a shovel. He was probably the most stubborn man who has ever walked this planet, and he finished the house in just a couple of years.

When I was born, my parents had just bought the cabin from my grandparents and I came to spend every summer there. I was an only child, so one could think that it must have been boring to spend so much time in the woods, with only a few friends to play with in the same village. But it was not. With the forest on one side of the house and the lake on the other, there was always something to explore.

In the spring, when we came back to the cabin after the winter, there were frogs everywhere. They were mating at the bottom of the lake and I remember finding this so fascinating, since they were never there otherwise. The next time we visited, there were tadpoles everywhere. I caught a few and kept them in a bucket (the eight-year-old me did not know better...). I learned that they developed their legs first, before their tails disappeared and they became tiny frogs. For a little kid, this was extremely exciting. I intended to keep the tiny frogs as pets, but one morning almost every single frog had escaped from my bucket. I guess it taught me that nature has its own will and you cannot control it, no matter how much you want to.

We spent every summer in the cabin. We went home from time to time to do the laundry, shower properly and to check the mail. And of course, so I could see my friends. For someone who is used to having an entire lake to herself, going to public beaches was not much fun. But that was what my friends did, and when I was at home I had no other choice. It was crowded, there were no fish to see when swimming, and I just wanted to go back to the calm lake in the woods. I realized at a young age how extremely lucky I was to have that place to go to – where I could run barefoot in summer meadows, pick strawberries in the garden and go to bed with wet hair after an evening swim.

Early mornings have always been my favourite time of day. Even as a teenager. Sneaking out at 5 o'clock in the morning with my camera was the absolute best thing to do – watching the sun rise and nature waking up, observing and documenting it, saving those moments as memories close to my heart.

I remember one particular morning very well. I had been out on one of my early-morning wanderings and was on my way back to the cabin.

I was walking up a steep hill and I couldn't really see what was at the top. When I reached the top I found myself face to face with a deer. The sun was rising behind it and it just stood there, in the middle of a thousand sun beams, and looked at me. This moment felt like an eternity, but it probably only lasted a few seconds. After looking into each other's eyes, the deer turned and jumped into the forest. I felt so at one with nature in that moment: just two beings meeting on a morning walk, living side by side in a place they both love, so very different from each other, yet so incredibly alike.

I have spent hundreds of mornings out walking with my camera, and I have probably spent just as many sitting on a rock by the lake, watching the "fairy dance". I have always loved the thought of the fog being dancing fairies (the Swedish word *älvdans*, which means mist or fog, directly translates as "fairy dance"). It makes the whole thing even more beautiful. Everything is silent, except for a fish or two, and a crane trumpeting somewhere in the woods.

At the cabin, the days always feel longer than when at home. It probably has something to do with all the fresh air, but also the fact that you do different things than at home. You live with nature in a totally different way than when living in the city. On a stormy day you might need to get rid of a tree that has fallen over the only road leading to your house. Another day you might have to get up in the middle of the night to get rid of water in the basement. Some days are just for laying in the grass and watching the clouds pass by, reading a book and taking a nap (or two). With no internet, no TV, no washing machine and no schedule to follow, you have more time. Time to just be. Time

to explore what is around you. Notice things you would not see otherwise. It is like taking a step back from modern life and everything that is going on in the world. Your world is around you. It's what you see, what you smell, what you feel.

Even though I couldn't be on vacation and live without a washing machine every day of the year, these small breaks in the countryside have taught me so much about nature and life. Living close to nature has given me a lot of respect for it, and an intense love for it. I know that nature has a lot to give, if I want it. I am free to roam the forests, swim in the lakes, sit on mountain tops and pick berries, mushrooms and flowers. Nature is generous, but we cannot just take without giving something back. What we could give back is love – love, and a will to take care of the natural world around us, for it belongs here just as much as we do. No one and nothing can own something that cannot be tamed or controlled.

Treat nature and wildlife with respect. Take no more than you need (foxes and bears like fresh berries, too). Leave nothing behind. When you leave, there should not be a trace of you, except your footprints. Leave enough flowers for the bumblebees and butterflies. Observe the ant hill, but do not touch it; thousands of ants spent their lives building it. Release the fly instead of killing it. Watch your step in the forest – you might step on what could become a big tree one day. Open your eyes and ears and take in the beauty of everything around you: a bird singing, autumn leaves in bright colours, the first cherry blossoms or water droplets on a beautiful flower. It is all there for you to see; you just have to open your eyes.

I could run barefoot in summer meadows, pick strawberries in the garden and go to bed with wet hair after an evening swim.

BLUEBERRY CHEESECAKE

BLÅBÄRSCHEESECAKE

This semi-frozen blueberry cheesecake makes the mind wander off
to the forest – to that smell of pine and old trees, to the quietness,
to the stained fingertips and the buckets full of tiny blue treasures.
Just a handful of blueberries will give this cake the most
wonderful purple colour.

SERVES 8–12

12–15 caramel cookies (page 203)

75g (2½oz/5 tbsp) vegan
    margarine, melted

250g (9oz/2 cups) cashew nuts

300ml (10½fl oz/1¼ cups) full fat
    coconut milk

50g (1¾oz/scant ½ cup)
    blueberries, plus extra for
    decorating

Finely grated zest of 1 lemon

3 tbsp lemon juice

4 tbsp maple syrup

¼ tsp pure vanilla powder,
    or 1 tsp vanilla bean paste

Crush the cookies using a pestle and mortar, or put them in
a food bag and carefully whack them with a rolling pin, until
they resemble a coarse rubble. Transfer the cookie crumbs to
a bowl and add the melted margarine. Mix thoroughly.

Press the cookie mixture into the base of a 20cm (8in)
springform cake tin in an even layer. Place in the fridge to
firm up while you prepare the filling.

Put the remaining ingredients in a blender or food processor
and blitz until smooth.

Remove the tin from the fridge and pour the filling over the
base. Gently tap the tin against the countertop to remove any
air bubbles and to ensure a smooth, even surface.

Cover the tin with cling film (plastic wrap) and freeze for at
least 6 hours.

About 10 minutes before serving, take the cheesecake out
of the freezer, remove it from the tin and allow it to sit at
room temperature.

Just before serving, decorate the top of the cheesecake with
some fresh blueberries, then slice and serve.

SUMMER PAVLOVA WITH BERRIES

SOMMARPAVLOVA MED BÄR

On warm summer days, I'm generally not in the mood for heavy desserts. A simple pavlova with lots of fresh berries is a perfect compromise when you want something sweet that's light yet delicious.

SERVES 6

FOR THE PAVLOVA

150ml (95fl oz/scant⅔ cup) aquafaba

135g (4¾oz/⅔ cup) caster (superfine) sugar

1 tbsp lemon juice

¼ tsp pure vanilla powder, or 1 tsp vanilla bean paste

FOR THE TOPPING

200ml (7fl oz/scant 1 cup) vegan whipping cream

250g (9oz/2 cups) fresh berries (I like to use strawberries and blueberries)

Icing (confectioner's) sugar, for dusting

Preheat the oven to 120°C/250°F/Gas ½ and line a baking sheet with baking parchment.

Using a hand-held electric whisk, beat the aquafaba in a large mixing bowl until stiff peaks begin to form.

Begin adding the sugar in a slow and steady stream, while still beating the mixture, until you have a stiff, glossy meringue. Add the lemon juice and vanilla and beat until combined. At this stage the meringue should be pretty solid, and if you turn the bowl upside down the meringue should hold itself in the bowl. If it doesn't look like it's quite there, then beat for a little longer.

Spoon the meringue into a large circle or rectangle onto the prepared baking sheet, ensuring that the edges of the meringue are slightly higher than the middle.

Bake for 1½ hours in the lower part of the oven, then turn off the oven and leave the meringue to cool fully inside (in the oven). This will take at least 2 hours.

When the meringue has cooled, carefully remove it from the baking parchment and transfer it to a platter.

Pour the whipping cream into a medium bowl and beat with a hand-held electric whisk until fluffy. Evenly dollop the whipped cream into the dip of your meringue and then top with fresh berries. Just before serving, give everything a generous dusting of icing sugar.

TIME IS ONE OF THE FEW THINGS YOU CANNOT KEEP FOR TOMORROW

For people living in the modern world, time is a scarce commodity. Many of us live a stressful lifestyle and it can feel like all we do is work, eat, sleep, repeat. Since so many of us live like this, it's easy to think that this is the way it has to be.

With full calendars and full-time jobs, there is not much time for cooking dinner, reading to our kids, helping out with homework and just relaxing. Our days are filled with activities and we run around from one to the next. Why? Because we want to, or because we are supposed to? For whom do we do it?

Often, we are too busy to reflect on how we live our lives. We work harder and we take work home with us. We have smartphones that keep us updated 24/7 and let us know about every new email in our inbox. And when we stop working, there is social media, TV, the news… The list goes on. We always have something to occupy ourselves with, and many of us never reflect on what we do with our time. Yet, so many are complaining about always being tired and stressed out.

To start questioning the lifestyle many of us live is not easy. We want to be seen to be as active and busy as our friends are; we want to have a nice home and the latest clothes. But why? Often,

I believe, it is to show others (who really don't care) that we are successful. We don't want to appear less important than anyone else. But since when did "things" and a hectic lifestyle define our value? Exhaustion is not a status symbol. What is anything worth if you are not truly happy and satisfied with your life? If you constantly try to find ways to be more efficient and save time, it is probably time for a change.

In a world where bigger is better and more is more, how can you get away with less? The key is to stop thinking about others and start thinking about you. No one knows how to live your life – except you. Whatever makes you happy is where you are heading. If you want change, you have to figure out why you want it, and what you do – and do not – want to have in your life. Most of us want more time – more time for the things we truly love to do, and more time for our families and friends.

The beautiful thing is that it is all connected. If you want more time, maybe you could work fewer hours? But you need the money to pay for all of life's expenses, I hear you say. But do you, really? What if you stopped buying new curtains, new clothes and new cars? Then you wouldn't need all that money, and maybe you could in fact work less. As grown-ups in the modern world, we have everything we need. In fact, we have way

When we stop chasing new things and instead start appreciating and taking care of what we already have, we do not only free up space in our homes and lives, but also in our heads.

more than we need. We own so much that we end up needing extra storage in which to keep all our things! In reality you don't need more storage or to organize your home better – you need less stuff.

In order to free up more time, take a look at what you are spending your time on. The average person spends more than three hours watching TV every day. That is three hours that could be spent reading, playing with your kids, or just talking. Slow living is about spending our time more wisely. Be out in nature, without your phone, breathe, explore and play. Make time to cook good food for yourself and your family.

We have to realize that we will never find the perfect pair of jeans, the perfect trip, the perfect anything. Because when we think we have found it, something better shows up – and on it goes. When we stop chasing new things and instead start appreciating and taking care of what we already have, we do not only free up space in our homes and lives, but also in our heads. When we are no longer occupied with looking for the next thing that will bring us temporary happiness, we can start working to become happy for real.

I think the key is to create a home, and a life, that we don't want to, or need to, run away from. This doesn't mean living a boring life away from society – it's about being present, spending your time well and taking a step back to think about what's really important in life.

Because you know what? The best things in life aren't things.

"ETT GOTT SKRATT FÖRLÄNGER LIVET."

"A hearty laugh lengthens your life."

BLUEBERRY CRUMBLE MUFFINS

BLÅBÄRSMUFFINS MED SMULDEG

Blueberry muffins meet blueberry crumble. These soft muffins are
filled to the brim with blueberries and topped with a crunchy layer
of crumble. The best of both worlds, and the perfect way to
showcase this wonderful forest berry.

MAKES 12 MUFFINS

100ml (3½fl oz/scant ½ cup)
   aquafaba

45g (1½oz/scant ¼ cup) caster
   (superfine) sugar

75g (2½oz/5 tbsp) vegan
   margarine

100ml (3½fl oz/scant ½ cup)
   plant milk

180g (6¼oz/1⅓ cups) plain
   (all-purpose) flour

2 tsp baking powder

Pinch of salt

200g (7oz/1½ cups) blueberries,
   fresh or frozen

FOR THE CRUMBLE

40g (1½oz/scant ½ cup)
   rolled oats

60g (2oz/scant ½ cup) plain
   (all-purpose) flour

45g (1½oz/scant ¼ cup) caster
   (superfine) sugar

50g (1¾oz/3½ tbsp) vegan
   margarine, diced

Preheat the oven to 180°C 350°F/Gas 4 and line a 12-hole
muffin tray with paper cases.

Put all the ingredients for the crumble into a large bowl
and use your fingertips to rub everything together until it
resembles a crumbly dough. Set aside for later.

Put the aquafaba and sugar in another large bowl and beat
with a hand-held electric whisk until white and fluffy.

Melt the margarine in a small saucepan set over a low heat,
then stir in the plant milk. Pour this into the aquafaba and
sugar mixture and stir to combine.

In a separate bowl, combine the flour, baking powder and
salt, then gently fold this into your wet mixture until no clumps
of flour are visible. Finally, add the blueberries and stir briefly
to evenly distribute.

Divide the batter evenly between the 12 paper cases then
sprinkle some of the crumble mixture over each muffin.
Bake in the middle of the oven for 12−15 minutes until
risen and golden.

Remove from the oven and allow the muffins to cool on
a wire rack before serving.

PLUM AND ALMOND GALETTE

PLOMMONGALETTE MED MANDEL

When I was a kid, my best friend had a huge plum tree in her garden. We used to climb that tree, sit on the top branches and eat plums until our stomachs hurt. Since then, I have always said that plums are best enjoyed fresh, straight from the tree, but this galette has made me rethink that statement…

SERVES 6

180g (6¼oz/1⅓ cups) plain (all-purpose) flour, plus extra for dusting

1 tbsp caster (superfine) sugar

Pinch of salt

150g (5½oz/⅔ cup) vegan margarine, chilled

2–3 tbsp ice cold water

Oat milk, for brushing

50g (1¾oz/heaped ½ cup) flaked (slivered) almonds

FOR THE FILLING

500g (1lb 2oz) fresh plums

70g (2½oz/⅓ cup) caster (superfine) sugar

¼ tsp pure vanilla powder, or 1 tsp vanilla bean paste

2 tbsp lemon juice

1 tbsp potato starch

To make the dough, combine the flour, sugar and salt in a large bowl. Dice the cold margarine and rub it into the flour using your fingertips until the mixture resembles breadcrumbs. Add the ice cold water, 1 tablespoon at a time, until the dough just comes together, then form it into a ball with your hands.

Shape the dough into a disc, wrap in cling film (plastic wrap) and let it rest in the fridge for at least one hour. Leaving it overnight is absolutely fine too. You may need to let the dough warm up for a few moments on the countertop before you start baking with it, to ensure that it's workable.

Preheat the oven to 200°C/400°F/Gas 6 and line a baking sheet with baking parchment.

On a lightly floured surface, roll out the dough to a circle about 3mm (⅛in) thick. Transfer it to the prepared baking sheet.

Cut the plums in half and remove the pit. Slice each plum half and place them in a large bowl. Add the remaining filling ingredients to the bowl and toss everything together to coat the plums.

Arrange the plum slices in a single layer in a pretty pattern on top of the dough, leaving a 4cm (1½in) border around the edge. Fold the bare edge of the dough over the plum filling and gently press to seal.

Brush the edges of the galette with oat milk, sprinkle with the flaked almonds, then place it in the middle of the hot oven and bake for about 35 minutes until the edges are golden brown and the plums are soft.

Remove from the oven, allow to sit for a few moments before serving warm or cold.

STRAWBERRY LEMONADE

JORDGUBBSLEMONAD

I love coffee, but even I don't drink it on the warmest summer days.
Instead, I spend the days in the shade sipping on ice cold strawberry
lemonade, preferably with a good book in my hand. The strawberries
add a fruity sweetness to the lemonade, which I absolutely love.

MAKES 6 SERVINGS

10 organic unwaxed lemons
270g (9½oz/1⅓ cups) caster
   (superfine) sugar
10 strawberries
Ice cubes
Mint leaves

Fill a large saucepan with 1 litre (35fl oz/4¼ cups) of water.

Cut the lemons into wedges and squeeze the juice into
the saucepan, then place the squeezed lemon wedges into
the pan too.

Bring the liquid to a boil, then add the sugar. Allow to boil
for 5 minutes.

Turn off the heat and allow to cool completely, then pour into
clean glass bottles. Store in the fridge until it's time to serve.

To serve, put the lemonade and strawberries into a blender
and blitz until smooth.

Pour into six glasses and add ice cubes and a couple of fresh
mint leaves to each glass.

LIFE IS TOO SHORT TO ALWAYS HAVE CLEAN FINGERNAILS

Nothing is so forgiving, yet so rewarding, as gardening. There are no rights and wrongs, and there is certainly no one right answer on how to succeed. It is like a lifelong experiment where you get to try, re-evaluate, then try again and again.

Like always, you cannot rush nature. Nature does what it wants, when it wants. Gardening requires a lot of patience, which is probably why most people find it so relaxing. There's something special about nurturing the ground, taking care of tiny plants and watching them grow into tall, steady ones that eventually bring you beautiful flowers or baskets full of produce. It is almost like watching a child grow up.

Gardening has given me so much respect for food and how it is grown. To see with your own eyes how much time and effort is needed to produce just a few baskets of beans and vegetables is so inspiring. You learn everything that can go wrong, what happens to the plants during a heavy downpour, and how devastating a long drought can be. And with that knowledge, the reward feels even greater when you get to harvest enough food to make an entire meal for your family. When you get so much you cannot even eat it all and have to freeze or preserve it in some way, you feel like the richest person on earth.

What can come out of only a few seeds is astonishing. Planting a handful of squash seeds in March can bring you all the squash you will need for the entire summer season. Probably even enough to preserve and enjoy for the majority of the autumn season too. A few berry bushes in the corner of your garden can bring you enough berries to last the entire winter.

To grow a garden requires work. Your hands will be dirty and so will your clothes. But there is no greater reward than seeing the work you've done turn into something that will fill your stomach or decorate your home. Life is too short to care about some dirt. The beautiful thing is that you get to decide how much time and effort you want to put in to your gardening. One thing is for sure though, every minute you spend will bring you happiness.

Another thing that makes gardening even more rewarding is that a garden only becomes more and more beautiful over the years. Older gardens often have a lot of old fruit trees. These old trees are not just extraordinarily beautiful to look at, they also provide us with fruit during autumn. It takes time for the trees to get this big, which makes them a real treasure in a garden.

One thing to remember is that a garden would be nothing without buzzing bees and butterflies. With few flower meadows left for these creatures to thrive in, it becomes more and more important to make our gardens insect friendly. It is not difficult at all – build a few insect hotels (google is your friend), place a few tiny rocks on a tray of water for bees to land on so they can drink, and grow a diverse range of flowers for them to feed on. Also, welcome birds, hedgehogs and other small animals into your garden. Let it be a place for everyone, and your garden will thrive.

You don't even need a garden to grow things. A balcony will do just fine, and even a windowsill can bring you a lot of fresh produce. Dare to try. Start small, see where it takes you and remember: you have to fail before you can master it.

HOW TO ENJOY YOUR OUTSIDE SPACE

+ Create a cosy space outdoors where you can eat breakfast, enjoy a cup of coffee, read a book or just sit and relax. A couple of chairs, a table and a few pillows are all you need. If possible, create a few different inviting spaces so you can move around throughout the day, depending on if you want shade or sunshine.

+ Try growing a few different vegetables, herbs or berries. You don't need a garden for this; a lot of edible things can be grown on a balcony or even on a windowsill. Harvesting fresh vegetables that you've grown yourself is so rewarding and, indeed, my version of luxury.

+ Surround yourself with plants and beautiful flowers. My personal favourites are dahlias, peonies, poppies, sweet peas and garden cosmos. Again, a lot can be grown on a balcony.

+ Put some string lights between two trees, on a porch or on the balcony. A simple trick to add cosiness to your outdoor space.

+ I love to start my day outside. Breathing the kind of fresh air that only exists in the early morning fills me with energy and makes me ready for the new day.

RASPBERRY AND CARDAMOM MUFFINS

MUFFINS MED HALLON OCH KARDEMUMMA

If my husband were to design recipes, he would make them 90 per
cent fruit, ten per cent dough. This is what I had in mind when
I created these muffins – lots of raspberries wrapped inside a soft
cake that tastes of freshly ground cardamom.

MAKES 12 MUFFINS

100ml (3½fl oz/scant ½ cup)
aquafaba

70g (2½oz/⅓ cup) caster
(superfine) sugar

75g (2½oz/5 tbsp) vegan
margarine

100ml (3½fl oz/scant ½ cup)
plant milk

180g (6¼oz/1⅓ cups) plain
(all-purpose) flour

2 tsp baking powder

1 tsp ground cardamom

200g (7oz/1½ cups) raspberries

Preheat the oven to 180°C/350°F/Gas 4 and line a 12-hole
muffin tin with paper cases.

Put the aquafaba and sugar in a large bowl and beat with
a hand-held electric whisk until white and fluffy.

Melt the margarine in a small saucepan set over a low heat,
then stir in the plant milk. Pour this into the aquafaba and
sugar mixture and stir to combine.

In a separate bowl, combine the flour, baking powder and
ground cardamom, then gently fold this into your wet mixture
until no clumps of flour are visible. Finally, add the raspberries
and stir briefly to evenly distribute.

Divide the batter evenly between the 12 paper cases and
bake in the middle of the oven for 12–15 minutes until risen
and golden.

Remove from the oven and allow the muffins to cool on a wire
rack before serving.

CHOCOLATE MERINGUES
WITH WHIPPED CREAM

CHOKLADMARÄNGER MED GRÄDDE

These chocolate meringues are like mini pavlovas. Made with really
dark chocolate and served with whipped cream, cocoa and… more
chocolate. You can also use this recipe to make bite-sized meringues
to serve with ice cream.

SERVES 6

100g (3½oz) dark chocolate
 (70% cocoa solids or higher),
 plus 25g (1oz), to serve

150ml (5fl oz/scant ⅔ cup)
 aquafaba

135g (4¾oz/⅔ cup) caster
 (superfine) sugar

1–2 tbsp lemon juice

150ml (5fl oz/scant ⅔ cup) vegan
 whipping cream

Cocoa powder, to dust

Icing (confectioner's) sugar,
 to dust

Preheat the oven to 120°C/250°F/Gas ½ and line a baking
sheet with baking parchment.

Place your chocolate in a small heatproof bowl set over a pan
of barely simmering water. Once melted, give it a stir and place
to one side to cool slightly.

Using a hand-held electric whisk, beat the aquafaba in a large
mixing bowl until stiff peaks begin to form.

Begin adding the sugar in a slow and steady stream, while still
beating the mixture, until you have a stiff, glossy meringue.
Add the lemon juice and beat until combined. At this stage the
meringue should be pretty solid, and if you turn the bowl upside
down the meringue should hold itself in the bowl. If it doesn't
look like it's quite there, then beat for a little longer.

Carefully pour the cooled, melted chocolate over the meringue
and stir a couple of times to create streaks and swirls of
chocolate in the meringue (do not mix in fully).

Spoon six dollops of meringue on the prepared baking sheet,
each about 12cm (4½in) in diameter.

Bake in the lower part of the oven for 1½ hours, or until the
meringues easily peel away from the paper. Turn off the oven
and leave the meringues to cool completely in the oven. This
will take at least 2 hours.

Pour the whipping cream into a medium bowl and beat with
a hand-held electric whisk until fluffy.

Place the cooled meringues on plates, add a generous spoonful
of whipped cream to each, then grate over some dark chocolate
and dust with cocoa powder and icing sugar before serving.

COFFEE AND CHOCOLATE ICE CREAM

GLASS MED KAFFE OCH CHOKLAD

This creamy ice cream with bits of dark chocolate and a touch of coffee is one of my favourites. Making your own ice cream takes a little time, but it's not difficult. It's a no-churn recipe, which means that you don't need an ice cream machine to make it. All you need is a hand-held electric whisk and a freezer.

The condensed milk recipe makes a little more than you need for the ice cream, but can be stored in the fridge in a clean jar for just over a week and used for drizzling over ice cream or cake (like you would with caramel sauce).

MAKES ABOUT 1 LITRE (35OZ)

FOR THE CONDENSED MILK

1 litre (35fl oz/4¼ cups) soy milk

5 tbsp caster (superfine) sugar

Pinch of pure vanilla powder, or ½ tsp vanilla bean paste

300ml (10½fl oz/1¼ cups) vegan whipping cream

250g (9oz/1 cup) vegan condensed milk (see below for homemade)

60g (2oz/½ cup) icing (confectioner's) sugar

100g (3½oz) dark chocolate

3 tbsp really strong coffee

First, make the condensed milk. Combine all the ingredients in a large saucepan. Bring to a boil, then reduce the heat and simmer for about an hour. During this time you need to stir the mixture continuously to prevent it catching – this is extra important nearer the end of the cooking time, when the mixture has thickened. Your condensed milk is done when the liquid is reduced by two-thirds. Remove from the heat and allow to cool; it will thicken even more when cooling. Store in a clean, sealed container in the fridge for up to 10 days.

To make the ice cream, firstly beat the vegan whipping cream in a large bowl using a hand-held electric whisk until soft peaks form.

Add 250g (9oz/1 cup) of the condensed milk to the cream, then sift in the icing sugar. Beat for another couple of minutes until fully combined.

Place half the chocolate in a small heatproof bowl set over a pan of barely simmering water. Once melted, give it a stir and allow it to cool slightly before pouring it into your cream mixture. Add the strong coffee, then chop the remaining chocolate into small chunks and add this too.

Stir to just combine, then pour the mixture into a freezable container, seal and place in the freezer for at least 4 hours.

ICE CREAM SANDWICHES

SANDWICHGLASS

When you can't decide if you want cookies or ice cream, have both!
Put a generous layer of your favourite ice cream between crunchy
chocolate chip cookies and you have a decorative and
delicious dessert.

MAKES 8 SANDWICHES

125g (4½oz/½ cup plus 1 tbsp) vegan margarine, at room temperature

60g (2oz/5 tbsp) coconut sugar

45g (1½oz/scant ¼ cup) soft brown sugar

180g (6¼oz/1⅓ cups) plain (all-purpose) flour

½ tsp baking powder

Pinch of salt

Pinch of pure vanilla powder, or ½ tsp vanilla bean paste

3 tbsp aquafaba

100g (3½oz) dark chocolate, coarsely chopped

Vanilla ice cream (page 83), chocolate and coffee ice cream (page 124), or store-bought ice cream, to assemble

To make the cookies, preheat the oven to 200°C/400°F/Gas 6 and line a baking sheet with baking parchment.

Using a hand-held electric whisk, cream together the margarine, coconut sugar and soft brown sugar in a large bowl.

In a separate bowl, combine the flour, baking powder, salt and vanilla powder, then add this to your creamed mixture and stir to combine.

Add the aquafaba and chopped chocolate pieces, then stir again to ensure everything is combined.

Divide the cookie dough into 16 balls and place them, well spaced apart, onto the prepared baking sheet. Bake in the middle of the oven for 10–15 minutes, or until golden brown. Allow them to cool completely on the baking sheet, then store in an airtight container until needed.

To make ice cream sandwiches, place one scoop of ice cream between two cookies and press together slightly. If you are not eating the sandwiches right away, you can place them on a tray in the freezer until ready to serve.

[SLOW LIVING]

FORAGING FOR WILD TEA

Nature offers a great variety of tea ingredients; leaves, berries, herbs and flowers are delicious when dried and used for tea. It is also a very easy way to conserve summer and enjoy it during the winter months. There are a few things to think about when harvesting ingredients for your own tea.

Firstly, and most importantly, make sure that the plants you gather are not toxic. If you are unsure, leave it be. If you are on medication, make sure that it is safe to consume herbal teas. You can never be too careful.

HARVESTING

When harvesting ingredients for tea, it's best to do it just before noon on a sunny day. Plants contain essential oils and the levels of these oils are the highest before noon. If the plants are wet from fog, rain, or dew, the drying process will take longer, which is why it's better to harvest on a sunny day, when the dew is gone. For this reason, do not rinse your leaves, simply shake them to get rid of any unwanted guests.

Where possible, always choose fresh, seasonal ingredients. This helps to optimize the flavour of the tea.

DRYING LEAVES, HERBS AND FLOWERS

Drying requires patience. It's preferable to dry your herbs and leaves somewhere non-humid, where the temperature doesn't exceed 40°C/104°F. Keep this in mind if you want to use a dehydrator or oven to dry plants. If you have an attic, that is a perfect place for drying plants, but any dry place in your house will work just as well, as long as the plants are hidden from direct sunlight.

If your leaves or herbs have stems, you can loosely bind about ten stems together with string or yarn and hang them, with their heads down, from a hook, nail or beam. Make sure that there is space between the bunches. If you are drying individual leaves or flowers, place them separated on a wire rack, or on a clean, dry towel or piece of paper and place somewhere dry and warm. The drying process can take quite some time. Some plants only require a couple of days, while others require weeks. Touch the dried leaves or petals with your fingers – they should be very brittle and fall apart between your fingers. Try to remove the leaves from the stems without crushing them. Store in airtight glass jars protected from light.

Leaves to dry: blackcurrant, raspberry, strawberry, blackberry, birch.

Herbs to dry: mint, thyme, sage.

Flowers to dry: apple blossom, lilac, rose, lavender, cornflower.

DRYING FRUIT

Rinse the fruit and remove any seeds, pits and stems. Slice it into evenly sized pieces and place on a baking sheet lined with baking parchment. Make sure that the pieces aren't touching each other. Dry in an oven set to 50°C/122°F for 6–12 hours. Apples, pears and peaches need about 6 hours to dry, whereas lemon and orange peel need about 10 hours. It also depends on the thickness of the slices and the water content of the fruit, so adjust the time as needed. Once out of the oven, leave the fruit on the baking sheets overnight before placing in airtight glass jars. If they have dried out enough, they will keep indefinitely.

Fruits to dry: apples, pears, apricots, peaches, lemons, oranges, rhubarb.

DRYING BERRIES

Berries are best dried in the oven. Heat the oven to 50°C/122°F and place the berries on a baking sheet lined with baking parchment. Dry in the oven for 12–25 hours. They are ready when shrivelled and chewy. Stored in an airtight container these will keep for at least a year, but probably much longer.

Berries to dry: strawberries, raspberries, blueberries, blackcurrants, lingonberries.

Combining berries with their leaves makes a very tasty tea. By doing so, the flavour has more depth.

You can also use freeze-dried fruits and berries for making tea, if you prefer.

SPICES

Adding spices to your tea mix is a great idea. For Christmas, combine cloves, crushed cinnamon sticks, dried ginger, cardamom pods and dried orange peel for a warming combination that is just perfect for the holidays.

TURNING NATURE INTO TEA

The best thing about making your own tea is that you can create your favourite flavour combinations. There is no right and wrong. Dare to experiment and try new things. Store each ingredient separately and try new combinations every day. When you have found your favourite combination, you can prepare a mixed jar of it so you always have it to hand.

To make the tea, put 1 tablespoon of dried ingredients in a tea diffuser in a mug or cup (for a single serving), or put 1 tablespoon per person in a tea pot. Pour hot water (about 80°C/176°F, not boiling) over the tea and leave to brew for 5–10 minutes before enjoying.

A Few Tasty Combinations

+ Raspberry leaves, dried raspberries, blackcurrant leaves, dried strawberries

+ Blackberry leaves, dried blackberries, dried blueberries

+ Dried rhubarb, strawberry leaves, dried strawberries

+ Dried apple, crushed cinnamon sticks, dried ginger, apple blossoms, cornflowers

+ Mint and sage leaves

+ Camomile, mint, ginger, dried lemon peel

AUTUMN *höst*

SWEDISH BUTTERKAKA

BUTTERKAKA

Butterkaka combines all of my favourite flavours to eat in autumn.
Cinnamon buns are lined up next to each other and filled with soft
vanilla custard. This is best when eaten the same day as it is made,
but if you want to save it for later, pop it in the fridge.

SERVES 10

FOR THE BUNS

40g (1⅓oz/2½ tbsp) vegan
  margarine, plus extra for
  greasing

125ml (4½fl oz/½ cup)
  plant milk

15g (½oz) fresh yeast
  (or 7g/¼oz dried yeast)

25g (1oz/⅛ cup) caster
  (superfine) sugar

Pinch of salt

1 tsp ground cinnamon

210g (7½oz/1½ cups) plain
  (all-purpose) flour, plus extra
  for dusting

FOR THE CUSTARD

150ml (5fl oz/scant ⅔ cup)
  oat milk

1 tbsp potato starch

pinch of salt

½ tsp pure vanilla powder,
  or 2 tsp vanilla bean paste

2 tbsp caster (superfine) sugar

10g (⅓oz/2 tsp) vegan margarine

Melt the margarine in a small saucepan set over a low heat,
then stir in the plant milk. Let the liquid cool until it's lukewarm
(about 37°C/99°F).

Crumble the yeast into a large bowl, then pour over the
lukewarm milk and stir until the yeast is completely dissolved.

Add the sugar, salt, cinnamon and about two-thirds of the flour
to the bowl. Stir together until well combined and then work the
dough in the bowl with your hands for about 5 minutes, dusting
over the remaining third of the flour as you knead. You're
aiming for a smooth and slightly sticky dough. Shape the dough
into a ball and nestle it into the bottom of the bowl, then cover
the bowl with a tea (dish) towel and pop it in a warm place to
prove for about 45 minutes.

To make the custard, combine the oat milk and potato starch in
a saucepan set over a medium heat. Cook, stirring continuously,
until it thickens. Remove the saucepan from the stove and add
the salt, vanilla, sugar and margarine. Stir well until everything
has been incorporated, then set aside to cool completely.

Prepare the filling by mixing together the margarine, sugar and
cinnamon in a small bowl. Set aside.

On a lightly floured surface, roll out the dough to a large
rectangle measuring 30 x 25cm (12 x 10in). Spread the filling
evenly over the dough. Starting from a long edge, roll the dough
into a log, with the filling encased inside. Use a sharp knife or
a dough scraper to cut the roll into 10 even slices.

CONTINUED...

CONTINUED...

FOR THE FILLING

40g (1⅓oz/2½ tbsp) vegan
 margarine, at room temperature

15g (½oz) caster (superfine) sugar

½ tbsp ground cinnamon

FOR THE TOPPING

Plant milk, for brushing

Pearl sugar, granulated sugar
 or chopped almonds

Grease a 20cm (8in) round cake tin with vegan margarine
or line with baking parchment.

Arrange your cinnamon bun slices in the tin, cut side up, but
remember to leave a little space between them so there is room
for them to rise (if your buns won't all fit, place any extras on
a baking sheet lined with baking parchment).

Loosely cover the tin (and the baking sheet, if using) with a tea
towel and leave to prove for another 30 minutes. Meanwhile,
preheat the oven to 200°C/400°F/Gas 6.

Once risen, use your fingers to make a small hole in the middle
of each bun. Pipe or spoon some custard into each of the holes.

Brush the buns with plant milk and sprinkle with pearl sugar,
granulated sugar or chopped almonds.

Bake for 30 minutes in the lower part of the oven, or until
golden brown (any extra buns on a baking sheet will take a little
less time).

Remove your *butterkaka* from the oven and allow it to cool in
the tin before serving. The cake is best when enjoyed the same
day, but you can store it in the fridge for a couple of days, and
it also freezes quite well.

CHOCOLATE CAKE

CHOKLADTÅRTA

Chocolate cake works every season of the year, but it is especially good
during the darker months when there is less fresh produce available.
This cake is filled with the softest chocolate filling and decorated with
fluffy chocolate cream. Everything a chocolate lover could ask for.

SERVES 8–12

150ml (5fl oz/scant ⅔ cup)
  aquafaba
180g (6¼oz/scant 1 cup) caster
  (superfine) sugar
150g (5½oz/⅔ cup) vegan
  margarine, plus extra for
  greasing
200ml (7fl oz/scant 1 cup) oat milk
40g (1½oz/5 tbsp) cocoa powder
300g (10½oz/2¼ cups) plain
  (all-purpose) flour
1 tbsp baking powder

FOR THE FROSTING

150g (5½oz/⅔ cup) vegan
  margarine
120g (4¼oz/1 cup) icing
  (confectioner's) sugar
250g (9fl oz/1 cup plus 2 tbsp)
  vegan cream cheese
20g (⅔oz/2½ tbsp) cocoa powder

FOR THE TOPPINGS

100g (3½oz) dark chocolate
100ml (3½fl oz/scant ½ cup)
  vegan whipping cream

Preheat the oven to 180°C/350°F/Gas 4 and grease and line
a deep, round cake tin 15–18cm (6–7in) in diameter, with
a depth of at least 10cm (4in).

Beat the aquafaba and sugar in a large bowl using a hand-held
electric whisk until white and fluffy.

Melt the margarine in a small saucepan set over a low heat,
then stir in the oat milk. Pour this into the aquafaba and sugar
mixture and stir to combine.

In a separate bowl, combine the cocoa powder, flour and baking
powder, then gently fold this into the wet mixture until you
have a smooth batter.

Pour the batter into the prepared tin and bake in the middle of
the oven for 40–50 minutes. Remove from the oven and allow
the sponge to cool completely in the tin.

To make the frosting, add the margarine to a large bowl and sift
in the icing sugar. Beat until light and fluffy, then add the cream
cheese and cocoa powder and beat again until smooth and
combined. Pop the frosting in the fridge for about 15 minutes
to firm up.

Once the sponge is cool, remove it from the tin and carefully
cut it horizontally into three even layers using a serrated knife.

Place a sponge layer on a cake stand or plate. Spread a layer
of frosting on top, then add your next sponge layer. Spread
another layer of frosting over the second sponge and then top
the cake with your final sponge layer. Using a palette knife,
cover the top and sides of your cake with the remaining frosting.

Place the cake in the fridge while you prepare the toppings.

CONTINUED...

CONTINUED...

Place your chocolate in a small heatproof bowl set over a pan of barely simmering water. Once melted, give it a stir and place to one side to cool slightly.

Place the whipping cream in a medium bowl along with a generous tablespoon of the melted chocolate. Beat using a hand-held electric whisk until stiff peaks form, then transfer the chocolate cream to a piping bag fitted with a star nozzle.

Take the cake from the fridge and drizzle the reserved melted chocolate around the top edge of the cake, encouraging it to drip over the edge every now and again. Next, pipe little mountains of chocolate cream around the top edge of the cake.

Store the cake in the fridge until it's time to serve.

CINNAMON APPLE WREATH

KANELKRANS MED ÄPPELFYLLNING

This wreath is inspired by cinnamon buns, but with an apple sauce filling. Apple trees are the most common garden tree where I live. Many of us have more apples than we can eat, so making apple sauce is a great way to preserve them. The recipe for the apple sauce makes more than you'll need for this wreath – store the remainder in the fridge and use to top your morning oatmeal.

SERVES ABOUT 12

75g (2½oz/5 tbsp) vegan margarine

250ml (9fl oz/1 cup) plant milk, plus extra for brushing

25g (1oz) fresh yeast (or 12g/½oz dried)

90g (3oz/scant ½ cup) caster (superfine) sugar

¼ tsp salt

2½ tbsp ground cinnamon

420g (15oz/scant 3¼ cups) plain (all-purpose) flour, plus extra for dusting

300g (10½oz) apple sauce (see below for homemade)

Pearl sugar, granulated sugar or chopped almonds, for sprinkling

FOR THE APPLE SAUCE (MAKES ABOUT 600G/21OZ)

1kg (2lb 4oz) apples

100g (3½oz/½ cup) caster (superfine) sugar

First, make the apple sauce. Peel, core and quarter the apples, placing them in a bowl of cold water as you go to prevent browning. Drain the water and place the apples in a large saucepan. Add 50ml (1¾fl oz/3½ tbsp) water to the pan and bring to the boil. Cook and stir until the apples have softened, then add the sugar. Bring back to the boil then take off the heat and allow to cool. Once cool, mash with a fork, or blitz in a blender to create a smooth sauce. Pour into clean jars then store in the fridge.

Melt the margarine in a small saucepan set over a low heat, then stir in the plant milk. Let the liquid cool until it's lukewarm (about 37°C/99°F). Crumble the yeast into a large bowl, then pour over the lukewarm milk and stir until the yeast is dissolved.

Add 45g (1½oz/scant ¼ cup) of the caster sugar, the salt, ½ tablespoon of the cinnamon and about two-thirds of the flour to the bowl. Stir until well combined and then work the dough in the bowl with your hands for about 5 minutes, dusting over the remaining third of the flour as you knead. You're aiming for a smooth and slightly sticky dough. Shape the dough into a ball and nestle it into the bottom of the bowl, then cover with a tea (dish) towel and pop it in a warm place to prove for about 45 minutes.

On a floured surface, roll out the dough to a rectangle measuring 25 x 60cm (10 x 23½in). Spread apple sauce over the rectangle and sprinkle with the remaining caster sugar and cinnamon. Fold the dough in half lengthwise, cut the rectangle lengthwise into three equally thick slices, then braid the three slices into a plait. Line a baking sheet with baking parchment and transfer the braid onto it. Shape the braid into a wreath by simply joining the ends together. Cover again and allow to prove for another 30 minutes. Meanwhile, preheat the oven to 200°C/400°F/Gas 6.

Brush the wreath with plant milk and sprinkle with pearl sugar, granulated sugar or chopped almonds. Bake in the lower part of the oven for about 20–30 minutes, or until golden brown. Allow to cool slightly then serve warm with coffee.

PEAR TART

PÄRONTARTE

Apples are probably the most popular autumn fruit, and pears tend to be forgotten. Pears are in fact delicious in both cakes and pies; this pear tart has a caramelly flavour thanks to the maple syrup, and goes perfectly with the vanilla ice cream on page 83.

SERVES 6–8

180g (6¼oz/1⅓ cups) plain (all-purpose) flour, plus extra for dusting

1 tbsp caster (superfine) sugar

Pinch of salt

150g (5½oz/⅔ cup) vegan margarine, chilled

1–3 tbsp ice cold water

Oat milk, for brushing

FOR THE FILLING

2–3 pears

2 tbsp maple syrup

2 tbsp raw cane sugar

1 tsp ground cardamom

To make the pastry, combine the flour, sugar and salt in a large bowl. Dice the cold margarine and rub it into the flour using your fingertips until the mixture resembles breadcrumbs. Add the ice cold water, 1 tablespoon at a time, until a dough just comes together, then form it into a ball with your hands.

Shape the dough into a disc, wrap in cling film (plastic wrap) and let it rest in the fridge for at least one hour. Leaving it overnight is absolutely fine too. You may need to let the dough warm up for a few moments on the countertop before you start baking with it, to ensure that it's workable.

Preheat the oven to 200°C/400°F/Gas 6 and line a baking sheet with baking parchment.

On a lightly floured surface, roll out the dough to a rectangle about 3mm (⅛in) thick. Transfer it to the prepared baking sheet.

Cut the pears in half and remove the cores. Thinly slice the pear halves and place them in a bowl. Add the other filling ingredients and toss everything together to coat the fruit.

Arrange the pear slices overlapping slightly on top of the pastry, leaving a 4cm (1½in) border around the edge. Fold the bare edge of the dough over the pear filling and gently press to seal.

Brush the edges of the tart with oat milk, then place it in the middle of the hot oven and bake for about 35 minutes until the edges are golden brown and the pears are soft.

Remove from the oven and allow to sit for a few moments before serving warm or cold.

LINGONBERRY ROLL CAKE

RULLTÅRTA MED LINGON

This roll cake is not just delicious, it is also very pretty. The tangy lingonberry filling balances the otherwise rather sweet cake. If you prefer, you can use raspberries, strawberries or blueberries instead.

SERVES 12

50ml (1¾ fl oz/3½ tbsp) rapeseed (canola) oil

75ml (2½ fl oz/5 tbsp) aquafaba

175ml (5½ fl oz/scant ¾ cup) plant milk

210g (7½ oz/1½ cups) plain (all-purpose) flour

60g (2oz/⅓ cup) potato starch

110g (3¾ oz/heaped ½ cup) caster (superfine) sugar, plus extra for sprinkling

2½ tsp baking powder

Pinch of salt

¼ tsp pure vanilla powder, or 1 tsp vanilla bean paste

200ml (7fl oz/scant 1 cup) lingonberry jam (see page 50 for homemade), or use a jam of your choice

Lingonberries, to decorate

Icing (confectioner's) sugar, for dusting

Preheat the oven to 180°C/350°F/Gas 4. Line a Swiss roll (jelly roll) baking tin with baking parchment.

In a large bowl, combine the oil, aquafaba and plant milk (if using vanilla paste, add it at this stage too). Beat using a hand-held electric whisk until fluffy.

In a separate bowl, combine the flour, potato starch, sugar, baking powder, salt and vanilla (if using powder). Sift into the wet mixture and gently fold to combine.

Pour the batter into the prepared tin and spread evenly, then bake in the middle of the oven for about 20 minutes, until the sponge is just firm but springs back to the touch.

Remove from the oven and allow to cool in the tin for 5 minutes.

Place a new sheet of baking parchment on the countertop and sprinkle with some caster sugar. Turn the sponge out onto the baking parchment (with the top of the cake face down on the sugar), then gently peel away the baking parchment that lined the tin.

Trim the edges of the sponge so that you have an even rectangle, then spread the lingonberry jam evenly over the top.

Starting at a short edge, roll up the sponge into a log, using the baking parchment to help you. Place on a serving plate, decorate with fresh lingonberries and dust with icing sugar before serving.

APPLE PIE

ÄPPELPAJ

Apples are one of my favourite fruits, since you can use them for so many different things. Pie is, of course, one of the most popular things to make, which is totally understandable as pies are beautiful as well as delicious. Eating a slice of this pie is like tasting a piece of autumn.

SERVES 6–8

FOR THE PASTRY

270g (9½oz/2 cups) plain (all-purpose) flour, plus extra for dusting

2 tbsp caster (superfine) sugar

Pinch of salt

½ tsp ground cinnamon

200g (7oz/¾ cup plus 2 tbsp) vegan margarine, chilled

3–5 tbsp ice cold water

Plant milk, for brushing

FOR THE FILLING

1kg (2lb 4oz) apples

25g (1oz/1½ tbsp) vegan margarine

90g (3¼oz/scant ½ cup) caster (superfine) sugar, plus 1 tbsp extra for sprinkling

2 tsp ground cinnamon

Pinch of salt

1 tbsp lemon juice

1 tbsp cornflour (cornstarch)

Vanilla ice cream (page 83) or custard (page 136), to serve

To make the pastry, combine the flour, sugar, salt and cinnamon in a large bowl. Dice the cold margarine and rub it into the flour using your fingertips until the mixture resembles breadcrumbs. Add the ice cold water, 1 tablespoon at a time, until a dough just comes together, then form it into a ball with your hands.

Shape the dough into a disc, wrap in cling film (plastic wrap) and let it rest in the fridge for at least one hour. Leaving it overnight is absolutely fine too. You may need to let the dough warm up for a few moments on the countertop before you start baking with it, to ensure that it's workable.

Meanwhile, make the filling. Peel and core the apples, then thinly slice.

Melt the margarine in a large saucepan set over a medium heat. Add the apple slices, sugar, cinnamon, salt and lemon juice and stir to coat. Bring to a boil then simmer for 3–5 minutes, or until the apples begin to soften.

Sprinkle with the cornflour and stir to combine, then simmer for another couple of minutes, or until the filling begins to thicken. Remove from the heat and allow to cool completely.

Preheat the oven to 200°C/400°F/Gas 6.

Divide the dough into two portions, one a little bigger than the other. On a lightly floured surface, roll out the larger portion of the dough to a circle about 3mm (⅛in) thick. Use this to line a 20cm (8in) pie dish, then place this in the fridge while preparing the other portion of dough.

Cut the remaining dough portion in half again, then roll one half into a 3mm (⅛in) thick rectangle that's about 30cm (12in) long. Cut the dough lengthwise into 6 even strips.

Remove the pie dish from the fridge and fill it with the cold apple filling.

CONTINUED...

CONTINUED...

You're now going to create the lattice crust – this is easier than it might seem. Place 3 of the pastry strips on top of the pie, evenly spaced apart. Fold the two outer strips all the way back and place one of the unused strips horizontally across the pie. Refold the strips back down.

Now, fold back the middle pastry strip and place another strip horizontally on top of the pie. Refold the middle strip so that it covers the second horizontal strip. Fold back the two original outer strips again and place your last pastry strip on top of the pie. Refold the strips and you should have a lattice pattern.

Crimp and seal the edge of the pie using a fork, then trim off any excess pastry.

With your final portion of pastry, roll it into a sausage shape using your hands, then roll out into a long, narrow rectangle 3mm (⅛in) thick and at least 1½ times the length of the circumference of your pie dish. Carefully divide this pastry strip lengthwise into three equal strips, then braid together to create a plait (sometimes I find this easier to do in smaller lengths, then I join them together on the pie). Carefully transfer the plait to your pie dish and arrange in a ring around the outer edge of the pie. Press down very lightly to stick.

If you have any excess pastry, you can re-roll it and cut out some pretty leaf shapes to decorate the centre of the pie.

Brush the entire pie crust with plant milk and sprinkle some sugar on top.

Bake the pie in the lower part of the oven for about 20 minutes, then lower the heat to 175°C/350°F/Gas 4 and bake for another 45 minutes until golden.

Remove from the oven, allow to stand for 10–15 minutes, then serve with vanilla ice cream or custard.

CARDAMOM BUNS

KARDEMUMMABULLAR

This will forever be my favourite recipe. No baked treat in the world
can beat a freshly baked cardamom bun enjoyed with a cup of coffee.
If you want, you can use cinnamon instead of cardamom,
or why not try a combination of both?

MAKES ABOUT 40

FOR THE BUNS

150g (5½oz/⅔ cup) vegan
margarine

500ml (17fl oz/2 cups) plant milk

50g (1¾oz) fresh yeast
(or 25g/1oz dried)

45g (1½oz/scant ¼ cup) caster
(superfine) sugar

½ tsp salt

1 tsp ground cardamom

780g (1lb 7oz/6¼ cups) plain
(all-purpose) flour, plus extra
for dusting

Plant milk, for brushing

Pearl sugar, granulated sugar or
chopped almonds, to sprinkle

FOR THE FILLING

150g (5½oz/⅔ cup) vegan
margarine, at room temperature

45g (1½oz/scant ¼ cup) caster
(superfine) sugar

2 tbsp ground cardamom

To make the buns, melt the margarine in a small saucepan set
over a low heat, then stir in the plant milk. Let the liquid cool
until it's lukewarm (about 37°C/99°F).

Crumble the yeast into a large bowl, then pour over the
lukewarm milk and stir until the yeast is completely dissolved.

Add the sugar, salt, cardamom and about two-thirds of the
flour to the bowl. Stir together until well combined and
then work the dough in the bowl with your hands for about
5 minutes, dusting over the remaining third of the flour as you
knead. You're aiming for a smooth and slightly sticky dough.
Shape the dough into a ball and nestle it into the bottom of the
bowl, then cover the bowl with a tea (dish) towel and pop it in
a warm place to prove for about 45 minutes.

Meanwhile, prepare the filling by mixing together the
margarine, sugar and cardamom in a small bowl. Set aside.

Line two or three large baking sheets with baking parchment
(or arrange 40 cupcake cases on the baking sheets).

Divide the dough in half. On a lightly floured surface, roll out
the first dough portion into a large rectangle measuring about
30 x 40cm (12 x 16in). Spread half of the filling evenly over the
rectangle. Now, fold the dough in half lengthwise so that you
have a rectangle measuring 15 x 40cm (6 x 16in). Cut 20 strips
of dough widthwise, each about 2cm (¾in) wide.

Pick up a strip, twist it a few times, then wrap it around two
fingers and tuck the loose end in at the bottom of the bun (see
photos overleaf for guidance). Place the bun on a lined baking
sheet (or in a cupcake case). Repeat with the remaining strips.

CONTINUED...

CONTINUED...

Repeat this process with the other half of the dough so that you have 40 buns.

Loosely cover your buns with a tea towel and leave to prove for about 30 minutes. Meanwhile, preheat the oven to 250°C/480°F/Gas 9.

Brush your buns with plant milk and sprinkle with pearl sugar, granulated sugar or chopped almonds.

Bake for about 10 minutes until golden brown (you may need to rotate the baking sheets so that they all bake evenly, or bake in batches). Keep an eye on the buns because they burn easily.

Remove from the oven, transfer to a wire rack to cool, then enjoy your buns with a cup of coffee.

CHOCOLATE PIE

CHOKLADPAJ

Traditionally, pies and tarts contain fruits and berries, but as the
saying goes, traditions are meant to be broken. At least when
they can be turned into something just as good, like a thick
and indulgent chocolate mousse.

SERVES 8–10

FOR THE PIE CRUST
180g (6¼oz/1⅓ cups) plain
(all-purpose) flour, plus extra
for dusting
1 tbsp caster (superfine) sugar
Pinch of salt
150g (5½oz/⅔ cup) vegan
margarine, chilled
2–3 tbsp cold water

**FOR THE CHOCOLATE
MOUSSE**
150g (5½oz) dark chocolate
(at least 70% cocoa solids),
plus extra for grating
150ml (5fl oz/scant ⅔ cup)
aquafaba
2 tbsp cocoa powder
1 tbsp caster (superfine) sugar

TO DECORATE
100ml (3½fl oz/scant ½ cup)
vegan whipping cream
Flaky sea salt

To make the pie crust, combine the flour, sugar and salt in
a large bowl. Dice the cold margarine and rub it into the flour
using your fingertips until the mixture resembles breadcrumbs.
Add the ice cold water, 1 tablespoon at a time, until a dough just
comes together, then form it into a ball with your hands.

Shape the dough into a disc, wrap in cling film (plastic wrap)
and let it rest in the fridge for at least one hour. Leaving it
overnight is absolutely fine too. You may need to let the dough
warm up for a few moments on the countertop before you start
baking with it, to ensure that it's workable.

Preheat the oven to 200°C/400°F/Gas 6 and grease a 20cm
(8in) pie dish.

On a floured surface, roll out the dough to a circle, about 5mm
(¼in) thick and a little bigger than your pie dish.

Carefully transfer the dough to the pie dish and use your fingers
to press it into the base and sides of the dish. Chill in the fridge
for 30 minutes.

Prick the pie crust with a fork, then bake for 20–30 minutes,
or until golden. Remove from the oven and leave to cool.

To make the chocolate mousse, melt the chocolate in a
heatproof bowl set over a pan of barely simmering water.

In a large bowl, beat the aquafaba until very fluffy and firm
using a hand-held electric whisk (if you turn the bowl upside
down it should stay put). Add the melted chocolate, cocoa
powder and sugar to the aquafaba and beat again to combine.

Pour the mousse into the cooled pie crust and spread evenly.
Place in the fridge for at least one hour.

In a medium bowl, whip the cream using a hand-held electric
whisk until fluffy. Transfer to a piping bag fitted with a star
nozzle, then pipe little mounds of cream all over the top of the
pie. Grate over some dark chocolate, sprinkle with a pinch of
flaky sea salt and serve.

CHOCOLATE COOKIES
WITH PEARL SUGAR
CHOKLADKAKOR

These were my favourite cookies as a kid. My mum used to make them
for Christmas every year. They are crispy and gooey at the same time,
and topped with pearl sugar for a sweet touch. They are delicious
when served with a cup of coffee.

MAKES 30 COOKIES

90g (3¼oz/scant ½ cup) caster
(superfine) sugar

150g (5½oz/1 cup plus 2 tbsp)
plain (all-purpose) flour, plus
extra for dusting

1 tsp baking powder

2 tbsp cocoa powder

¼ tsp pure vanilla powder,
or 1 tsp vanilla bean paste

100g (3½oz/7 tbsp) vegan
margarine, chilled

60g (2oz) pearl sugar

Preheat the oven to 180°C/350°F/Gas 4 and line two baking
sheets with baking parchment.

In a large bowl, combine the sugar, flour, baking powder, cocoa
and vanilla. Dice the cold margarine and rub it into the flour
using your fingertips until the mixture resembles breadcrumbs.
Bring the dough together using your hands, then turn it out
onto a lightly floured surface.

Divide the dough into two portions and roll each into a 2cm
(¾in) thick log. Transfer to the prepared baking sheets.

Flatten out the logs with your hands to form 2cm (¾in) thick
rectangles. Sprinkle the dough with the pearl sugar.

Bake in the middle of the oven for 10–15 minutes, or until
they've got a nice brown colour. Keep a close eye on them as
they burn easily.

Remove from the oven, allow to cool on the baking sheets for
a couple of minutes, then, while they are still warm and soft,
slice the logs widthwise on the diagonal to form cookies.

Let cool completely on the baking sheets (they'll crisp up as
they cool) then store in an airtight container.

CINNAMON BUN MUFFINS

KANELBULLEMUFFINS

Cinnamon buns are my favourite bake of all time, but it takes a while
to prepare them. For moments when you are short on time, yet can't
stop thinking about cinnamon buns, these cinnamon bun cupcakes
will be a life-saver. They take no more than 30 minutes to bake and
taste exactly like cinnamon buns. Well, almost.

MAKES 12 MUFFINS

100ml (3½fl oz/scant ½ cup)
   aquafaba
70g (2½oz/⅓ cup) caster
   (superfine) sugar
100g (3½oz/7 tbsp) vegan
   margarine
100ml (3½fl oz/scant ½ cup)
   plant milk
210g (7½oz/1½ cups) plain
   (all-purpose) flour
2 tsp baking powder
2 tsp ground cinnamon

FOR THE TOPPING

2 tsp ground cinnamon
1 tbsp raw cane sugar
Pearl sugar, to sprinkle

Preheat the oven to 180°C/350°F/Gas 4 and line a 12-hole
muffin tin with paper cases.

Put the aquafaba and sugar in a large bowl and beat with
a hand-held electric whisk until white and fluffy.

Melt the margarine in a saucepan over a low heat, then stir
in the plant milk. Pour this into the aquafaba and sugar mixture
and stir to combine.

In a separate bowl, combine the flour, baking powder and
cinnamon, then gently fold this into to the wet mixture.

Divide the batter between the cupcake cases.

For the topping, combine the cinnamon and raw cane sugar
and sprinkle a little on top of each muffin. Use the back of
a teaspoon to swirl the cinnamon sugar into the top of each
muffin, then sprinkle the tops with pearl sugar.

Bake in the middle of the oven for 12–15 minutes until light
golden. Remove from the tin and let the muffins cool on a
wire rack.

Serve or store in an airtight container for a couple of days.
These also freeze well.

THE AIR IS CRISP AND AUBURN LEAVES COVER
THE GROUND LIKE AUTUMN CONFETTI

[SLOW LIVING]

HOWLING WIND AND RAINDROPS ON A METAL ROOF

I love rain. I'm mesmerized by it. The sound of it, the feeling of it and the mood that comes with it. There is something about it that makes my heart warm and my soul calm. Sitting by the window on a dark and stormy night is one of the best things I know, and the sound of raindrops hitting a metal roof makes me relax instantly. So much so, that when I was about to give birth to my son, I listened to a playlist of raindrops hitting a metal roof, as that was the best thing to make me stay calm and get ready for what was ahead of me.

I also love to be outside when it rains. It makes me feel free. Your hair gets all messy, your clothes get wet and droplets fall from your eyelashes into your eyes. It doesn't matter. There is something about rain that makes all your senses come to life. The sharp raindrops that hit your bare cheeks in an autumn storm. The howling wind, trying to find its way through your clothes all the way to your skin. You cannot be somewhere else, because even if you try, those cold drops will bring you right back to the present.

I like the thought of rain being tiny pieces of the ocean falling down. And in a way it is. It is all connected. Water is never really created, it just changes its shape, moving from one place to another. The water we drink today is the same water that the dinosaurs and first humans on Earth drank thousands of years ago. It is for us to borrow, only to give it back from whence it came. The rain we feel on our outstretched hands could be the same water in which a baby polar bear went for its first swim. It could be the same as the water your grandchild will drink when tasting water for the first time. It is all connected. We are all connected.

To me, raindrops are the perfect lullaby; they are inspiration and art. Sadly, lots of people despise grey weather and heavy rain like it is a dangerous disease. But just like in life, there cannot only be sunny days. We need rain to thrive. Instead of waiting for the rain to pass, try dancing in it. Smell the light summer rain falling on dry soil, a scent that even has its own name, petrichor, which I find astonishingly beautiful. Watch the heavy autumn downpour, see the raindrops dance in the puddles. Listen to the rhythm of water hitting the window.

Just like you have to cry from time to time, so must the sky. And no matter where in the world you live, the sound of falling rain is the same.

Complaining about the weather will never help. No matter how grumpy you are, or how much you yell at the dark clouds, the weather will do as it pleases. Trying to see the beauty in it instead of cursing it will make everything easier, and a lot funnier.

"DET FINNS INGET DÅLIGT VÄDER,
BARA DÅLIGA KLÄDER."

*"There is no such thing as bad weather,
only bad clothes."*

BROWNIES

BROWNIES

I think there are as many versions of "the perfect brownie" as there
are human beings. This version is crunchy on top and very (very)
gooey on the inside. You can easily adapt the recipe to match your own
preferences — if you want your brownies very gooey, bake them for a
shorter time, whereas if you want them less gooey, you should aim for
a few minutes more in the oven than I've specified below.

MAKES 12 BROWNIES

150ml (5fl oz/scant ⅔ cup)
   aquafaba

180g (6¼oz/scant 1 cup) caster
   (superfine) sugar

150g (5½oz/1 cup plus 2 tbsp)
   plain (all-purpose) flour

40g (1½oz/5 tbsp) cocoa powder

2 tsp baking powder

½ tsp salt

100ml (3½fl oz/scant ½ cup)
   rapeseed (canola) oil

Preheat the oven to 200°C/400°F/Gas 6. Line a 20 x 20cm
(8 x 8in) baking tin with baking parchment.

Put the aquafaba and sugar in a large bowl and beat with a
hand-held electric whisk until white and fluffy.

In a separate bowl, combine the flour, cocoa powder,
baking powder and salt, then fold this into the aquafaba
and sugar mixture.

Add the oil and stir until you have a smooth batter. Pour the
batter into the prepared tin and bake in the middle of the oven
for 12–16 minutes. If you want a very gooey brownie, go for
the lower baking time, and if you prefer them less sticky, go
for a few more minutes in the oven.

Let the brownie cool in the tin before cutting into 12 pieces.

CARROT CAKE

MOROTSKAKSTÅRTA

Traditionally in Sweden, carrot cake is not really a cake – more like blondies made with grated carrot and seasoned with cinnamon and cardamom, then topped with a thick layer of frosting. It's very yummy, and this is my version of that bake in layer-cake form.

If you want to make a four-layer cake (as pictured), make two batches of the sponge and double the amount of frosting.

SERVES 8–10

150ml (5fl oz/scant ⅔ cup) aquafaba

180g (6¼oz/scant 1 cup) caster (superfine) sugar

60g (2oz/⅓ cup) potato starch

180g (6¼oz/1⅓ cups) plain (all-purpose) flour

2 tbsp ground cinnamon

1 tbsp ground cardamom

¼ tsp salt

¼ tsp pure vanilla powder, or 1 tsp vanilla bean paste

2 tsp baking powder

100ml (3½fl oz/scant ½ cup) rapeseed (canola) oil

150g (5½oz) carrots, peeled and grated

FOR THE FROSTING

150g (5½oz/⅔ cup) vegan margarine

120g (4¼oz/¾ cup plus 2 tbsp) icing (confectioner's) sugar

250g (9oz/1 cup plus 2 tbsp) vegan cream cheese

1 tsp ground cardamom

¼ tsp pure vanilla powder, or 1 tsp vanilla bean paste

Preheat the oven to 180°C/350°F/Gas 4 and grease and line a deep, round cake tin 15–18cm (6–7in) in diameter, with a depth of at least 10cm (4in).

Put the aquafaba and sugar in a large bowl and beat with a hand-held electric whisk until white and fluffy.

In a separate bowl, combine the potato starch, flour, spices, salt, vanilla and baking powder, then fold this into the aquafaba and sugar mixture.

Add the oil and grated carrots to the batter and stir until smooth.

Pour the batter into the prepared tin and bake in the lower part of the oven for 50–60 minutes until risen and golden. A skewer inserted into the centre of the cake should come out clean.

Allow the sponge to cool in the tin for 15 minutes, then remove from the tin and transfer to a wire rack to cool completely.

When completely cool, cut the cake in half horizontally with a serrated knife so that you get two even layers.

To make the frosting, place the margarine in a large bowl, sift over the icing sugar, then beat until light and fluffy using a hand-held electric whisk. Add the cream cheese, cardamom and vanilla and beat again until smooth.

Place a sponge layer on a serving plate. Cover with some of the frosting, then place the other sponge on top. Using a palette knife, cover the top and sides of the cake with the remaining frosting.

Place the cake in the fridge for about an hour before serving to allow the frosting to set and firm up.

WINTER

vinter

SWEDISH SAFFRON BUNS

LUSSEKATTER

These are soft buns rich in saffron flavour and decorated with raisins
at each end. I like to soak the raisins in mulled wine before decorating
the buns with them. Saffron buns are, in fact, very good when served
with mulled wine, too (see page 211). I freeze half the batch of buns as
soon as they're cooled so that I always have some on hand.

MAKES 40 BUNS

150g (5½oz/⅔ cup) vegan
margarine, plus extra, melted,
for brushing

500ml (17fl oz/2 cups) plant milk,
plus extra for brushing

1g (a pinch) saffron

135g (4¾oz/⅔ cup) caster
(superfine) sugar

50g (1¾oz) fresh yeast
(or 25g/1oz dried)

½ tsp salt

900g (2lb/6¾ cups) plain
(all-purpose) flour, plus extra
for dusting

80 raisins (2 raisins per bun)

100–200ml (3½–7fl oz/
scant ½–scant 1 cup) mulled
wine (see page 211 for
homemade), optional

Melt the margarine in a small saucepan set over a low heat,
then stir in the plant milk. Let the liquid cool until it's lukewarm
(about 37°C/99°F). Grind the saffron and 1 tablespoon of the
sugar using a mortar and pestle, then add it to the milk mixture.

Crumble the yeast into a large bowl, then pour over the
lukewarm milk and stir until the yeast is completely dissolved.

Add the remaining sugar, the salt and about two-thirds of the
flour to the bowl. Stir together until well combined and then
work the dough in the bowl with your hands for 5–10 minutes,
dusting over the remaining third of the flour as you knead.
You're aiming for a smooth and slightly sticky dough. Shape the
dough into a ball and nestle it into the bottom of the bowl, then
cover the bowl with a tea (dish) towel and pop it in a warm place
to prove for about 45 minutes.

Line two baking sheets with baking parchment. Tip the dough
out onto a lightly floured surface and work it for a minute or so.
Using your hands, roll the dough into a long sausage shape, then
cut it into 40 equal pieces.

With open palms, roll each piece of dough on the work surface
into a long sausage shape again, about 1cm (½in) in diameter.
Curl the ends of each in opposite directions, forming an "S"
shape. Place the buns on the prepared baking sheets and repeat
with the rest of the dough to make 40 buns. Leave some space
between them on the sheet. Loosely cover the buns again and
leave them to prove for a further 30 minutes.

Meanwhile preheat the oven to 220°C/425°F/Gas 7.

In a small bowl, cover the raisins in the mulled wine and leave
to soak while the buns are proving.

Brush the buns with melted margarine and press a raisin into
the swirls at each end. Bake one sheet of buns at a time in the
middle of the oven for about 10 minutes until golden. Remove
from the oven and transfer to a wire rack and loosely cover with
a tea towel to cool. Best eaten fresh.

SWEDISH SEMLOR

SEMLOR

These cardamom buns are filled with almond paste, then covered
with whipped cream before you put a lid on and sprinkle with
powdered sugar. Simple, and very delicious. In Sweden, *semlor* were
traditionally eaten on a particular day in February, called Fat Tuesday,
the day before Lent. Nowadays people eat *semlor* throughout the
entire month of February, but never during any other time of the year.

MAKES 12 BUNS

FOR THE BUNS

25g (1oz) fresh yeast
   (or 12g/½oz dried)

200ml (7fl oz/scant 1 cup) oat
   milk, plus extra for brushing

1 tsp cardamom seeds

45g (1½oz/scant ¼ cup) caster
   (superfine) sugar

Pinch of salt

75g (2½oz/5 tbsp) vegan
   margarine, at room
   temperature, diced

330g (11½oz/scant 2½ cups)
   plain (all-purpose) flour, plus
   extra for dusting

FOR THE ALMOND PASTE

100g (3½oz/1 cup) ground
   almonds (almond flour)

5 tbsp caster (superfine) sugar

Pinch of pure vanilla powder,
   or ½ tsp vanilla bean paste

TO FINISH

250ml (9fl oz/1 cup) vegan
   whipping cream

Icing (confectioner's) sugar,
   for dusting

Crumble the yeast into a large mixing bowl. Add the oat milk
and stir until the yeast is completely dissolved.

Grind the cardamom seeds using a pestle and mortar, then add
1 teaspoon of the ground spice to the milk mixture (reserve the
rest for your almond paste).

Now add the sugar, salt, margarine and about half the flour to
the mix. Work the dough for a few minutes until the margarine
is mixed in.

Add the rest of the flour and work the dough in the bowl with
your hands for at least 10 minutes (or 5 minutes if using a stand
mixer), until smooth. Shape the dough into a ball and nestle
it into the bottom of the bowl, then cover the bowl with a tea
(dish) towel and pop it in a warm place to prove for about
1 hour, or until it has doubled its size.

Prepare a large baking sheet lined with baking parchment.

Once proved, tip out the dough onto a lightly floured surface
and work it for a couple of minutes. Divide the dough into
12 evenly sized pieces and roll each piece into a round ball.

Carefully transfer the buns to the lined baking sheet, loosely
cover with the tea towel and leave to prove for another
30 minutes.

Meanwhile, preheat the oven to 220°C/425°F/Gas 7.

Brush the buns with oat milk and bake for 10–15 minutes,
or until golden brown. Transfer the buns to a wire rack and
allow to cool completely.

CONTINUED...

CONTINUED...

Using a small sharp knife, cut the "lids" off the buns by cutting downwards in a triangle shape, with the knife slightly angled towards the middle of the bun. Prise the triangular lids out of the buns and then use a teaspoon to scrape a small well in the centre of each bun. Reserve the crumbs and lids.

To make the almond paste, combine the ground almonds, sugar, vanilla and the reserved ground cardamom in a medium bowl. Add 2–3 tablespoons of cold water, a little at a time, until the mixture comes together to form a paste.

Add the reserved crumbs from the buns to the almond filling. If it becomes too dry, you can add a splash of the whipping cream to get the desired paste-like texture.

Using a teaspoon, fill the holes in the buns with the almond paste.

Using a hand-held electric whisk, beat the whipping cream until fluffy and firm. Pipe or spoon cream onto the top of each bun.

Place the lids back on top of the buns and dust with icing sugar before enjoying.

AUNT HARRIET'S GINGERBREAD COOKIES

TANT HARRIETS PEPPARKAKOR

When I grew up, my family always dedicated an entire day to baking gingerbread cookies and saffron buns. It was one of the best days of the year. I did, however, like the gingerbread cookie dough more than the actual cookies (to be honest, I still do). I've also made sure to maintain this tradition and I hope my son will have as sweet memories of this day as I have. The recipe is from the fifties and I got it from my mum, who got it from her mum. Traditions at their best.

MAKES 100 GINGERBREAD COOKIES (HALVE THE QUANTITIES IF NEEDED)

150g (5½oz/⅔ cup) vegan margarine, at room temperature

225g (8oz/1 heaped cup) caster (superfine) sugar

50ml (1¾fl oz/3½ tbsp) maple syrup

½ tbsp ground ginger

1 tbsp ground cinnamon

½ tbsp ground cloves

1 tsp ground cardamom

½ tbsp bicarbonate of soda (baking soda)

600g (1lb 5oz/4½ cups) plain (all-purpose) flour, plus extra for dusting

FOR THE ICING

120g (4¼oz/1 cup) icing (confectioner's) sugar

1½–2 tbsp lemon juice (or water)

In a large mixing bowl, combine the margarine, sugar and syrup and stir until smooth. Add 200ml (7fl oz/scant 1 cup) water, along with the spices and bicarbonate of soda. Gradually add the flour and stir until the mixture comes together as a dough.

Tip the dough out onto a lightly floured surface and knead until firm but a little sticky. Flatten the dough into a disc, wrap in cling film (plastic wrap) and place in the fridge overnight.

When you are ready to bake, preheat the oven to 220°C/425°F/Gas 7 and line two baking sheets with baking parchment.

Divide the dough into 4–6 pieces. Re-wrap all but one to keep them from drying out. Roll out the first portion of dough to a rectangle 2mm (1/16 in) thick.

Use cookie cutters to stamp out shapes and carefully transfer them to a lined baking sheet. Once the first baking sheet is full, bake in the middle of the oven for about 5 minutes until golden. Watch the cookies, as they burn very easily.

While the first batch of cookies is baking, continue to stamp out cookies to fill the second sheet. When the first tray is baked, remove the tray from the oven and allow to cool for a few minutes before transferring the cookies to a wire rack to cool completely. Put the second tray of cookies in the oven to bake while you roll out more dough and stamp out more cookies to refill the first tray. Repeat until all the dough is used.

To make the icing, combine the sugar and lemon juice in a small bowl until you have a thick, pipeable consistency. Transfer the icing to a piping bag fitted with a small round nozzle (or use a freezer bag with the corner snipped off), then pipe designs onto your cooled biscuits. Allow to set fully.

Stored in an airtight cookie tin, these will keep for up to a month.

SAFFRON AND ALMOND BISCOTTI

SAFFRANSBISCOTTI MED MANDEL

Biscotti are double-baked biscuits that can be varied according to the seasons. Here, I've flavoured them with saffron and bits of crispy almonds, which is perfect for the Christmas holidays. I like to mix things up and add chocolate and hazelnuts for rainy autumn days.

MAKES ABOUT 25

100g (3½oz/7 tbsp) vegan margarine

1g (a pinch) saffron

100ml (3½fl oz/scant ½ cup) plant milk

90g (3¼oz/scant ½ cup) caster (superfine) sugar

100g (3½oz/¾ cup) almonds, coarsely chopped

240g (8½oz/1¾ cups) plain (all-purpose) flour

1½ tsp baking powder

Flaked (slivered) almonds or pearl sugar, to decorate

Preheat the oven to 180°C/350°F/Gas 4 and line a baking sheet with baking parchment.

Melt the margarine in a small saucepan set over a low heat and add the saffron and plant milk.

In a mixing bowl, combine the sugar, chopped almonds, flour and baking powder, then add the melted margarine and milk mixture and mix to form a dough.

Divide the dough into two portions and roll each into a neat log measuring about 25cm (10in) long and 3cm (1¼in) wide. Transfer the logs to the prepared baking sheet and sprinkle with flaked almonds or pearl sugar.

Bake the loaves in the middle of the oven for about 25 minutes until firm then remove from the oven.

Lower the oven temperature to 125°C/250°F/Gas 1.

Cut the loaves widthwise into 1cm (½in) thick slices. Lay the slices on their sides on the baking sheet.

Return the biscotti to the oven for another 10 minutes until the slices are dry and crisp. Turn off the oven, but leave the biscotti inside until the oven is cold.

Stored in an airtight container, these will keep for up to a month, or you can freeze them.

[SLOW LIVING]

A SIMPLE HOME INSPIRED BY NATURE

Our home should have room for everything. It is the place where we eat, sleep, relax and play. Our entire lives should fit in there. Like gardening, there are no rights or wrongs when creating a home. The most important thing, the only important thing, is that you like it. What works for some, does not work for others.

I'm a minimalist at heart, and too much colour and too much stuff makes me stressed out. I want to surround myself with earthy tones, space and treasures from nature. Bringing nature inside adds a lot of calmness to a home, I believe. A fallen branch to place in a vase, a bouquet of dried grass and a few rocks in a jar. Furniture made from natural materials, like wood or stone, is beautiful and will last forever. The best thing about wood is that it gets better the older it is.

Textiles made from natural materials, like linen or cotton, will last much longer than synthetic ones and will bring a soft and calm feeling to your home. The thing about linen is that the messier and more wrinkled it is, the better it looks. Perfect if you, like me, aren't a big fan of ironing. Linen also gets better and better the more it is washed.

Glass and metal are other great choices when choosing materials. If treated right, they will last a lifetime. Like wood, metal only gets better as it ages, and it often gets a beautiful patina.

Keep in mind though, living a slow and simple life is not at all about redecorating your entire home to make it look like a picture-perfect house from a magazine or the internet. It is about surrounding yourself with only the things you need, and love. The most important thing is to get to know yourself, and your own style. You should forget about other people and what is trending at the moment. Your home is not for others to like; it is yours and you should love it. Surround yourself with things that make your heart smile.

"LAGOM"
Not too much, not too little. Just right.

IF YOU LIKE NATURAL MATERIALS AND
WANT A CALM HOME INSPIRED BY
NATURE, HERE ARE MY BEST TIPS:

+ *Natural is best* — Napkins, tablecloths
and curtains made from linen make your home
welcoming and calm. Also choose bedding
and towels made from organic cotton or linen
for softness and breathability.

+ *Handmade storage* — Handmade baskets
made of straw, bamboo and rattan are great
for storing things, and you'll be supporting
small makers in the process.

+ *Give life to old treasures* — Look for old
furniture at flea markets and antique stores;
here, you'll find unique things that reflect
your personality and style.

+ *Buy things only when you really need them* —
not buying things impulsively saves money,
makes your home less cluttered and is good for
the planet.

+ *A place for everything and everything in its
place* — put items where they belong to avoid
clutter and time spent looking for things.

+ *Avoid trends* — trends change and if you
follow them, you'll feel the need to constantly
change your home. Keep your own style and
you won't feel the need to renew all the time.

+ *Bring nature inside* — a bowl of autumn
leaves, cones, chestnuts and some candles
on a tray, or some garden flowers on the night
stand. A simple branch found in the forest
is beautiful to put in a vase and will last a
long time.

GINGERBREAD AND LINGONBERRY BUNDT CAKE

MJUK PEPPARKAKA MED LINGON

This soft cake tastes just like classic gingerbread cookies.
It is flavoured with warming spices like cinnamon, cloves and
cardamom. The lingonberries add a tartness to the otherwise
sweet cake, and the contrast is perfect.

SERVES 12

180g (6¼oz/1⅓ cups) plain
(all-purpose) flour

135g (4¾oz/⅔ cup) caster
(superfine) sugar

1½ tsp ground cinnamon

1 tsp ground cloves

1 tsp ground ginger

1½ tsp baking powder

75g (2½oz/5 tbsp) vegan
margarine, plus extra for
greasing

250ml (9fl oz/1 cup) plant milk

60g (2oz) lingonberries, plus extra
to decorate (if you can't get hold
of lingonberries use the same
quantity of dried cranberries,
or omit the berries completely)

Preheat the oven to 180°C/350°F/Gas 4 and grease a bundt
cake tin.

In a large bowl, combine the flour, sugar, ground spices and
baking powder.

Melt the margarine in a saucepan set over a low heat and add
the plant milk. Stir together briefly, then pour this into the bowl
with the dry ingredients and mix to combine. Carefully fold in
the lingonberries.

Pour the batter into the prepared tin and bake in the lower part
of the oven for about 40 minutes, until risen and slightly golden.
A skewer inserted into the centre of the cake should come
out clean.

Remove from the oven and allow to cool in the tin for about
15 minutes, then invert the cake onto a wire rack, remove the
tin, and leave to cool completely.

Decorate with lingonberries just before serving, if you like.

CHRISTMAS CAKE

JULTÅRTA

A tasty and Christmassy cake that is easy to make and can be decorated in lots of different ways. Soft ginger cake is paired with fluffy vanilla filling and decorated with gingerbread cookies. If you want a less sweet cake, try adding 1 teaspoon of dried lingonberry powder along with the filling ingredients and decorate with fresh or frozen lingonberries.

SERVES 8–12

FOR THE SPONGE

150ml (5fl oz/scant ⅔ cup) aquafaba

45g (1½oz/scant ¼ cup) caster (superfine) sugar

60g (2oz/⅓ cup) potato starch

180g (6¼oz/1⅓ cups) plain (all-purpose) flour

1 tbsp ground cinnamon

1 tbsp ground cloves

2 tsp ground cardamom

1 tbsp ground ginger

¼ tsp salt

¼ tsp pure vanilla powder, or 1 tsp vanilla bean paste

2 tsp baking powder

100ml (3½fl oz/scant ½ cup) rapeseed (canola) oil

FOR THE FILLING

200ml (7fl oz/scant 1 cup) vegan whipping cream

¼ tsp pure vanilla powder, or 1 tsp vanilla bean paste

30g (1oz/3½ tbsp) icing (confectioner's) sugar

Preheat the oven to 180°C/350°F/Gas 4 and grease and line a deep, round cake tin 15–18cm (6–7in) in diameter, with a depth of at least 10cm (4in).

To make the sponge, put the aquafaba and sugar in a large bowl and beat with a hand-held electric whisk until white and fluffy.

In a separate bowl, combine the potato starch, flour, ground spices, salt, vanilla and baking powder, then gently fold this into the aquafaba and sugar mixture.

Add the oil to the batter and stir until smooth.

Pour the batter into the prepared cake tin and bake in the lower part of the oven for 50–60 minutes until risen and golden. A skewer inserted into the centre of the sponge should come out clean.

Let the sponge cool in the tin for 15 minutes, then remove from the tin and transfer to a wire rack to cool completely.

Once cool, using a serrated knife, carefully cut the sponge horizontally into two even layers.

For the filling, place the cream, vanilla and icing sugar in a medium bowl and beat using a hand-held electric whisk until very firm – this usually takes about 10 minutes.

CONTINUED...

CONTINUED...

FOR THE FROSTING

250g (9oz/1 cup plus 2 tbsp)
 vegan cream cheese
¼ tsp pure vanilla powder,
 or 1 tsp vanilla bean paste
60g (2oz/½ cup) icing
 (confectioner's) sugar

TO DECORATE

Gingerbread Cookies (see page
 180) or lingonberries

Place one of the sponges on a serving plate or cake stand then spread the filling over. Top with the other sponge.

To make the frosting, place all the ingredients in a large bowl, and stir until combined. Using a palette knife, carefully coat the entire cake in an even layer of frosting. Leave the finish rustic (to mimic snow) or smooth the sides and top using a cake scraper.

While the frosting is still wet, carefully press gingerbread cookies onto the sides to surround the cake. You can even top the cake with a miniature gingerbread house. Scatter the top of the cake with lingonberries, if you like.

Place in the fridge for a couple of hours to set and then bring to the table and serve.

CARAMEL CANDIES

KOLA

These soft, chewy, melt-in-your-mouth caramels have the perfect balance of sweetness and saltiness. These are lovely to gift to friends and family throughout the year, but are especially good as Christmas treats. You can adapt these to suit your tastes — add cocoa powder for a chocolate version, or saffron for a variation that is great at Christmas.

MAKES ABOUT 50

50g (1¾oz/3½ tbsp) vegan margarine

270g (9½oz/heaped 2¼ cups) caster (superfine) sugar

100ml (3½fl oz/scant ½ cup) maple syrup

300ml (3½fl oz/1¼ cups) vegan whipping cream

½ tsp flaky sea salt

¼ tsp pure vanilla powder, or 1 tsp vanilla bean paste

VARIATIONS

To make chocolate caramels, add 3 tbsp cocoa powder

To make saffron caramels, add a pinch of powdered saffron

Line a 15 x 20cm (6 x 8in) baking tin with baking parchment.

Add all the ingredients for the candies to a large saucepan. Bring to a boil, then simmer over a medium heat until the caramel has reached 130°C/250°F. If you don't have a sugar thermometer, drop ½ teaspoon of the mixture into a glass of cold water, then scoop it out. If you can mould the caramel into a firm ball then the mixture is ready.

Pour the caramel into the lined tin, leave to cool for 10–15 minutes, then sprinkle some flaky sea salt on top. Allow to cool completely at room temperature — this takes about 4 hours.

Lift the caramel out of the tin using the baking parchment, then cut into bite-sized pieces using a sharp knife (dipping your knife into a mug of hot water can help the cutting process).

Individually wrap the caramel candies in small pieces of baking parchment and tie the ends with string.

Store at room temperature. They will be good for about a week.

CHOCOLATE BALLS

CHOKLADBOLLAR

Chocolate balls are underestimated little treats that are made entirely
without an oven. In other words, they are perfect to make when you get
unexpected guests or just want something delicious with your afternoon
coffee. The combination of coffee, sugar and chocolate is delicious.
Adding some sea salt to the batter balances them perfectly.

MAKES ABOUT 20

120g (4¼oz/scant 1¼ cups)
    rolled oats

90g (3¼oz/scant ½ cup) caster
    (superfine) sugar

¼ tsp pure vanilla powder,
    or 1 tsp vanilla bean paste

4 tbsp cocoa powder

Pinch of sea salt

100g (3½oz/7 tbsp) vegan
    margarine, at room temperature

3 tbsp strong coffee (cold)

Pearl sugar, shredded coconut or
    finely chopped nuts, to decorate

Put the rolled oats in a blender and blitz until you have a flour.

Tip the oat flour into a large bowl and add the sugar, vanilla,
cocoa powder and salt. Next, add the margarine and beat with
a wooden spoon until well combined.

Pour in the cold coffee and give everything a final mix to ensure
the coffee is evenly distributed.

Roll walnut-sized pieces of the dough between your palms
to create small, even balls. Place the pearl sugar, shredded
coconut, or chopped nuts in a shallow dish and then toss/roll
the chocolate balls in the dish to coat.

Store in the fridge for up to 5 days.

THE FROST DECORATES THE
WORLD WITH TINY DIAMONDS
AND ALL YOU CAN HEAR IS
THE SOUND OF YOUR SHOES
TOUCHING THE SNOW

THIN OAT COOKIES

HAVREFLARN

These cookies are not the most beautiful, but they are extremely tasty
— chewy, caramelly and super crispy around the edges. They are one
of the easiest cookies you can make, and probably one of the
most delicious too.

MAKES 15 COOKIES

75g (2½oz/5 tbsp) vegan
   margarine
70g (2½oz/⅓ cup) caster
   (superfine) sugar
50g (1¾oz/½ cup) rolled oats
45g (1½oz/⅓ cup) plain
   (all-purpose) flour
½ tsp baking powder
50g (1¾oz) dark chocolate,
   broken into pieces

Preheat the oven to 180°C/350°F/Gas 4 and line a baking sheet with baking parchment.

Melt the margarine in a small saucepan set over a low heat.

Combine the sugar and oats in a large bowl, pour over the melted margarine, then stir everything together.

In a separate bowl, combine the flour and baking powder, then tip this into the oat mixture and mix until there are no clumps of flour.

Spoon about 15 generous tablespoons of mixture onto the prepared baking sheet, ensuring you leave enough space between each to allow for spreading.

Bake in the middle of the oven for 10−12 minutes until golden around the edges. Keep an eye on them as they burn easily.

Remove from the oven and allow to cool completely on the tray.

Place the chocolate in a heatproof bowl set over a pan of barely simmering water. Once melted, give the chocolate a stir and take it off the heat. Dip each cookie halfway into the chocolate, then place back onto the lined tray, or on a wire rack set over a sheet of baking parchment.

Let the cookies set completely before enjoying. They will keep for up to 2 weeks in an airtight container. They also freeze well.

CARAMEL COOKIES

KOLAKAKOR

Caramel cookies are sweet, crunchy and chewy, easy to make and
loved by everyone. Personally, I think they always taste best eaten
outdoors when you need an energy boost during a hike in the forest,
or while perched on the front steps with your morning coffee,
listening to the birds sing.

MAKES 20–30 COOKIES

100g (3½oz/7 tbsp) vegan
  margarine, at room temperature

2 tbsp maple syrup

70g (2½oz/⅓ cup) raw cane sugar

¼ tsp pure vanilla powder,
  or 1 tsp vanilla bean paste

165g (5¾oz/1¼ cups) plain
  (all-purpose) flour

1 tsp baking powder

Preheat the oven to 180°C/350°F/Gas 4 and line a baking
sheet with baking parchment.

In a large bowl, cream together the margarine, maple syrup,
sugar and vanilla using a wooden spoon or hand-held
electric whisk.

In another bowl, combine the flour and baking powder, then
add this to the margarine and sugar mixture and stir to combine.

Divide the dough into two equal portions and roll each into
a log 30cm (12in) long. Transfer the logs to the prepared baking
sheet, leaving a generous amount of space between them.
Flatten out the logs with your hands to form rectangles 2cm
(¾in) thick.

Bake in the middle of the oven for 10–13 minutes until golden
around the edges.

Remove from the oven, allow to cool for a couple of minutes,
then, while they are still warm and soft, slice the logs widthwise
on the diagonal to form cookies.

Let the cookies cool completely, then store in an airtight
container for up to 2 weeks. They also freeze well.

COFFEE AND CHOCOLATE SQUARES

MOCKARUTOR

As the temperature drops and winter knocks on the door, there is less fresh produce available. Now is the time to turn to the saved jars of jam, to chocolate and nuts. These brownie bites are covered with a layer of the most delicious coffee and chocolate frosting you can imagine. Needless to say, these squares are perfect for cold winter days when the sun never really rises.

MAKES 12 SQUARES

150ml (5fl oz/scant ⅔ cup) aquafaba

180g (6¼oz/scant 1 cup) caster (superfine) sugar

150g (5½oz/1 cup plus 2 tbsp) plain (all-purpose) flour

40g (1½oz/5 tbsp) cocoa powder

2 tsp baking powder

½ tsp salt

100ml (3½fl oz/scant ½ cup) rapeseed (canola) oil

Shredded coconut, to sprinkle

FOR THE FROSTING

75g (2½oz/5 tbsp) vegan margarine

3 tbsp cocoa powder

3 tbsp strong coffee, cold

180g (6¼oz/1¼ cups) icing (confectioner's) sugar

Pinch of salt

Preheat the oven to 200°C/400°F/Gas 6 and line a 20cm (8in) square baking tin with baking parchment.

Put the aquafaba and sugar in a large bowl and beat with a hand-held electric whisk until white and fluffy.

In a separate bowl combine the flour, cocoa powder, baking powder and salt, then gently fold this into the aquafaba and sugar mixture.

Add the oil and stir until you have a smooth batter.

Pour the batter into the prepared tin and bake in the middle of the oven for 15–20 minutes until a skewer inserted into the centre comes out clean. Remove from the oven and allow to cool completely in the tin.

To make the frosting, melt the margarine in a saucepan set over a low heat, then add all the remaining ingredients to the saucepan. Beat until smooth.

Spread the frosting evenly over the cake, then generously sprinkle with shredded coconut. Leave to set at room temperature (or pop it in the fridge to speed up the process, if you prefer) then lift the cake out of the tin using the baking parchment and cut it into 12 squares.

HOT CHOCOLATE

VARM CHOKLAD

The beautiful thing about hot chocolate is that it is just as delicious enjoyed outdoors after a couple of hours of ice skating as it is indoors, snuggled up on the sofa with a good book. My favourite recipe contains lots of chocolate and is topped with whipped cream.

SERVES 2

5 tbsp vegan whipping cream
(or more to taste)
50g (1¾oz) dark chocolate,
plus 15g (½oz), grated, to serve
300ml (10½fl oz/1¼ cups)
plant milk
1 tsp cocoa powder, to dust

Place the whipping cream into a small bowl and beat using a hand-held electric whisk until fluffy and firm. Place to one side.

Put the chocolate in a saucepan with 100ml (3½fl oz/scant ½ cup) water and place over a low–medium heat until the chocolate has melted.

Add the plant milk and stir over a medium heat. As soon as it comes to the boil remove the pan from the heat.

Divide the hot chocolate between two mugs and top with the whipped cream. Dust with cocoa powder and sprinkle with some grated chocolate before serving.

GRANDPA'S RIS À LA MALTA

MORFARS RIS À LA MALTA

Eric was my grandfather. He was stubborn, had the strongest hands
(I'm sure he could break a rock if he wanted to) and smoked a tobacco
pipe. He was a train driver and could build anything. *Ris à la Malta*
was his favourite dessert. He never got to try my recipe, but I hope
he would have loved it. And I hope you will too.

SERVES 4

FOR THE RICE PUDDING

160g (5¾oz/¾ cup) short-grain
   or long-grain white rice

Pinch of salt

2 tbsp maple syrup

¼ tsp pure vanilla powder,
   or 1 tsp vanilla bean paste

1 cinnamon stick

800ml (28fl oz/3½ cups) oat milk

FOR THE RIS À LA MALTA

150ml (5fl oz/scant ⅔ cup) vegan
   whipping cream

300g (10½oz) cold rice pudding
   (see above)

1–2 tbsp icing (confectioner's)
   sugar

¼ tsp pure vanilla powder

2 oranges, peeled and thinly sliced,
   to serve

To make the rice pudding, put the rice and salt in a saucepan
with 400ml (14fl oz/1¾ cups) water. Bring to a boil, then lower
the heat, cover the pan and leave to cook for about 10 minutes.

Add the maple syrup, vanilla, cinnamon stick and oat milk, then
bring back to a boil.

Once it hits boiling temperature, reduce the heat so it's very
low, cover the pan and let the pudding slowly cook for about
30 minutes. Stir occasionally.

Once the rice is cooked and the liquid has been absorbed, turn
off the heat and remove the cinnamon stick. Allow the rice
pudding to cool completely.

To make the *ris à la Malta*, beat the cream in a large bowl using a
hand-held electric whisk until soft peaks form. Add the cold rice
pudding, icing sugar and vanilla and thoroughly stir to combine.

Spoon the *ris à la Malta* into small bowls and top with thin slices
of fresh orange to serve.

MULLED WINE

GLÖGG

Mulled wine is a classic Christmas drink in Sweden. You drink it warm
in tiny cups and serve it with raisins, almonds and Christmas bakes
like gingerbread cookies and saffron buns. When making mulled wine,
I recommend using a red wine with a milder flavour, since you
will add lots of spices and you don't want flavours from the
wine to interfere with them too much.

MAKES 18 SMALL SERVINGS

5 cinnamon sticks, plus extra
   to serve

20 cloves

1 piece of dried ginger (optional)

1 tsp ground cardamom

2 tsp dried bitter orange peel
   (or 1 large whole piece)

100ml (3½fl oz/scant ½ cup)
   vodka

70g (2½oz/⅓ cup) caster
   (superfine) sugar

1 x 750ml bottle of red wine

Break the cinnamon sticks into smaller pieces. Place the
cinnamon, cloves, dried ginger (if using), cardamom and bitter
orange peel in a jar and cover with the vodka. Leave on the side
to infuse for about 3 days (carefully shake the jar a couple of
times a day).

Strain the vodka mixture through a sieve and discard the spices.

Pour the vodka into a large bowl or jug (pitcher) and add the
sugar and red wine.

Now it's time to stir for quite a while. All of the sugar must
dissolve, or the *glögg* won't be good. Using a whisk, stir and
stir the mixture until all the sugar has dissolved and you can
no longer hear a rasping sound. I recommend that you then let
the *glögg* rest in the bowl for 10 minutes or so, then stir again.
At this point, if you still can't hear a rasping sound, then it's
ready. If you do still hear the sound of sugar against the sides
of the bowl when you whisk, stir again and repeat the resting/
mixing process until you can't hear anything.

Pour the mulled wine into clean, dry glass jars or bottles and
store in a dark cupboard for up to a month.

To serve, pour 50ml (1¾fl oz/3½ tablespoons) per person into
a saucepan and heat to 80°C/176°F. Pour into little heatproof
glasses or cups, add a cinnamon stick to each to garnish (if you
like) and enjoy.

WHEN YOU STOP AND LOOK
AROUND, YOU REALIZE THAT
BEAUTY IS EVERYWHERE

INDEX

TACK SÅ MYCKET

To Kalle, for putting up with me while making this book. Thank you for tasting everything, helping me improve the recipes and helping out with messy photo shoots. I couldn't have done this without you. You are my rock. I love you.

To Adam, for showing me what's important in life and for always putting a big smile on my face. You have taught me so much about life already. You are my everything.

To Harriet, my lovely editor – I'm beyond thankful for you. Thank you for believing in my ideas, for answering all my questions, and helping me create this book. *The Nordic Baker* would not be what it is without you. You are fantastic.

To Gemma for your incredible work with designing this book. You have read my mind from the start and you knew what I wanted before we even talked to each other. I'm so happy that I got to work with you. Thank you for creating the book of my dreams.

To family and friends for patiently tasting and evaluating recipes, and for always being there, encouraging and cheering.

To everyone who has followed me on social media and on the blog throughout the years. Thank you for all your messages, comments and support. This book would not exist without you. From the bottom of my heart – thank you. This book is for you.

To Becci, for making sure all the recipes and words were making sense, and to everyone at Quadrille who has been involved in creating *The Nordic Baker*. I'm so thankful for all of you.

ABOUT THE AUTHOR

Sofia Nordgren is a plant-based food blogger and photographer who runs the successful blog and Instagram The Nordic Kitchen, where she shares her delicious recipes mixed with tips and stories about living a Nordic lifestyle. She has been nominated for Best Food Photography in the Swedish Food Blog Awards 2017 and Grand Food Blog Award in the Swedish Food Blog Awards 2018.

Sofia lives with her family in a small city in the heart of Sweden. After studying to become a medical researcher, she then trained to be a nutritionist, before going after her dream of becoming a photographer. She loves early mornings, fog, coffee, old wood and the countryside. She has a passion for nature and slow, seasonal living and wants to inspire others to live a simpler life in harmony with nature.

PUBLISHING DIRECTOR Sarah Lavelle

JUNIOR COMMISSIONING EDITOR
  Harriet Webster

SENIOR DESIGNER Gemma Hayden

PHOTOGRAPHER Sofia Nordgren

FOOD & PROP STYLIST Sofia Nordgren

HEAD OF PRODUCTION Stephen Lang

PRODUCTION CONTROLLER Katie Jarvis

Published in 2021 by Quadrille,
an imprint of Hardie Grant Publishing

Quadrille
52–54 Southwark Street
London SE1 1UN
quadrille.com

Cataloguing in Publication Data: a catalogue
record for this book is available from the
British Library.

Text © Sofia Nordgren 2021
Photography © Sofia Nordgren 2021
Design © Quadrille 2021

ISBN 978 1 78713 714 1
Printed in China